Guildford - The Rock 'n' Roll Years

by

Nigel Enever

Cover Photograph: The Stormsville Shakers
Printed by: Caric Press Limited
Copyright: Nigel Enever 2009
Published by: Smudge Books, Survey House, 17-19 Neville Road, Peacehaven, East Sussex, BN10 8PE.

All rights reserved. No part of this book may be reproduced in any form or by any electronic or mechanical means, including information storage or retrieval systems, without permission in writing from the publisher, except by reviewer who may quote brief passages.

While the publishers have made every reasonable effort to trace the copyright owners of any or all of the photographs or quotations in this book, there may be some omissions of credits for which we apologise.

ISBN: 978-0-9564322-0-9

FOREWORD

Anyone, who like me, has a passion for history (and in my case local history) probably has one or two favourite periods in time in which they would either like to step back into, or would have liked to have lived in.

The 1960s is one that very much appeals to me. In fact, I was around at that time - but unfortunately I was just a child. How I wished I'd have been born 10 years earlier!

At the age of about five, I well recall watching The Beatles on the TV and saying that one day I would be a drummer like Ringo! I had an aunt who, unlike my parents, bought all manner of cool records. I remember her playing me The Rolling Stones' "Satisfaction" when it was released, and how she loved to play her copy of Sam the Sham and the Pharaohs' "Woolly Bully" on her small mono record player.

At such a young age I was being exposed to some great music from mainstream artists. However, being born and growing up in Guildford, at that time I had no idea that right on my doorstep there was such a vibrant music scene going on – all being enjoyed by a generation of young people who, to this day, I still think I would have liked to have been part of.

It was not until I picked up the guitar in the mid seventies and a few years later began to sing in local bands that I started to realise that something rather special had been going on in my home town just a decade before.

I soon started to hear stories about some of the local bands who had played the same venues I was playing, such as the Wooden Bridge and the Stoke Hotel. Names like the Stormsville Shakers were mentioned and that its singer, Phillip Goodhand-Tait, was now a solo recording artist and songwriter in the vein of the then quite new megastar Elton John.

As my interest in local history has expanded over the past 10 years, I thought I had a pretty good grasp of the Guildford music scene of the 1960s.

And then Nigel Enever came along with his idea for a book about it all. Straight away I realised that here was not only a platform to historically record the bands who were part of the local music scene at the time, but an important slice of local social history focusing on Guildford's young people was crying out to be recorded as well.

Nigel is just the person to have written this book – he was there at the time. Am I envious of him? You bet! Especially now I have read and learned so much more about what actually went on.

As a musician, I can appreciate the struggle Guildford bands had back then of making do with the quite basic instruments and amplification equipment that was only available to them.

But on the other hand, the sounds they were creating must have been fantastically raw as well as being very powerful – just the kind of stuff I like. Those who flocked to hear them, whether at the then new Civic Hall or in the clubs and the village halls in the local area would have been swept along with those heady sounds that, I guess, was all part of the UK's newly emerged youth generation – rebelling against their parents who still clung on to the dance band era.

I imagine, for many readers, this will be a nostalgic trip down the memory lane of their youth and early adult years. The names of the bands and their musicians plus the venues will evoke lots of memories.

It's not possible to bring back those times, but you can have a great time reminiscing and I am sure the music certainly plays on in those memories.

David Rose
Local historian and writer

Contents

	Introduction and Acknowledgements	
1.	Skiffle to Rock'n'Roll	1
2.	The Cranleigh and Godalming Connections	18
3.	Kossacks and Shakers	38
4.	Shakers become Circus	54
5.	The Venues	79
6.	The Music Shops	106
7.	'63-'65 - the Peak of the Beat Groups	127
8.	More Venues and Lifestyles	149
9.	Primevals and The Phantom Four	163
10.	Switch from The Rivals	181

Introduction and Acknowledgements

The Guildhall clock. The "cobbled" High Street. Iconic images of Guildford, but somewhere in that High Street was a club where music was made. In the environs of that High Street were the coffee houses, the youth clubs, the music shops where youngsters could gather to exchange idle gossip and listen to the latest sounds. In the schools and the front rooms and the bedrooms of houses in and around the Guildford area, chords would be plucked, words painstakingly learnt and poses struck. That identical things were happening all over Britain may not have occurred to these young Guildfordians. To them, this was a special time and a special place.

Many words have been written about sixties music and much about Guildford, but never have these two subjects been brought together in one volume until now. Guildford is the county town of Surrey and it is less than 30 miles from central London. At any one time in the mid-1960s, there were at least a dozen rock bands operating from within the old borough area and well over that number of venues at which they were able to perform.

This book is mainly concerned geographically with the old borough of Guildford and those small towns within its hinterland, to the south and west and particularly Godalming. It does not concern itself particularly with those more populated areas nearer London to the north and east, where such towns as Walton and Woking have spawned Status Quo and The Jam or Epsom (Jimmy Page) and Wallington (Jeff Beck). Nor those venues in the old north east part of Surrey at Richmond and Twickenham, from which such famous artists as The Rolling Stones and Eric Clapton emerged.

Guildford has a reputation for being within the stockbroker belt - certainly not a working-class town. Nonetheless, it has working-class areas within it, particularly to the north and west where there are large Council estates. Much as many rock artists would like to proclaim their working-class roots, many were educated at the better schools and universities. The art schools in particular were a prolific source of rock'n'rollers.

Looking back from my perspective of over 40 years and a career spent in the Chartered Surveying profession, I wonder what drove so many of my contemporaries to continue to strive for success in their chosen field of music for years after my faint hopes of such success had faded in my late teens. A genuine ability and interest in music is no doubt one of the reasons. There is, however, something of the instant hero in the fame, fortune and adulation which comes with such success, words which do not appear too often in the realms of Chartered Surveying or Accountancy!

I am not sure what motivated me to write this book. I have not lived in the Guildford area for many years and music has been nothing more than a hobby to me for most of my life. In 2003, however, I was called up by Stuart Reffold to play with The Switch at The Civic Hall "Stormsville" sixties reunion gig. It was a thrill to play there again and great to see old friends. I think it was this that must have sparked the idea.

It is now nearly two years since I started on the venture. I have made a number of trips around Surrey, Sussex and Hampshire interviewing the dramatis personae of the piece and who are quoted in this book. I have had telephone conversations with a number of others, including Dave Everson, Andy Latimer, Godfrey Matthews, Margaret Thomas, Bruce Bunker, Chris Ball, Jim Cook, Norman Harris and Debbie Broad. I would like to thank everyone for their help and co-operation and for the photographs and other memorabilia they have provided for use in the book. In particular I would like to mention Dave Brice, Mick Douglas, Peter Arthur, Terry Ward, Dick Middleton, Phillip Goodhand-Tait, Kirk Riddle, Ivor and Trish

Shackleton, Suzanne Martin, Dave Sherrington, David Rose, David Reading, Jim Cook, Chris Ball, Tony Backhurst, Betty Sherrington, Ian Latimer, Peter and Lee Anderton, Geoff Andrews, Stuart Reffold, John Enever, Ray and Sue Bradman, and, of course, the Surrey Advertiser. Also, Richard Batchelor of Caric Press, Andy Christou and David and Matt Enever for help with the production of the book .

I had an interesting tour on foot round Guildford with Suzanne Martin, visiting many of the places which were relevant to the story, in particular to see how some of the uses to which those buildings were put have changed or in some cases the buildings themselves.

I would particularly like to thank Suzanne, Phillip Goodhand-Tait and David Rose for going through drafts of the book, making grammatical and factual corrections and suggestions. I am sure that as a result of their efforts I am less likely to be sued for libel or defamation of character!

Phill was not sure about the project. He even compared it to synchronized swimming - it takes a long term to learn, but why do it! I do not pretend that Guildford is in any way unique. This is just a little bit of local history. Phill would have liked the book to have been funnier and sexier. The only problem is that I have had to remove or withhold some of the funniest and sexiest things I was told on my travels, for fear of embarrassing those involved and their loved ones.

Despite Phill's reservations, I have ploughed on, trawling the memories of those involved and my own recollections, together with archive material from the Surrey Advertiser and elsewhere and hope that you, the reader, will find something of interest in the following pages. If there are discrepancies, inaccuracies and inconsistencies in the book (as there no doubt will be), this is partly due to the fact that I have not been able to interview direct all the characters involved, some of the information is based on hearsay and, even in the case of those I have interviewed, inevitably after this period of time, the memory plays tricks.

Finally, a huge thanks to my wife, Lynn, for typing and re-typing the many drafts - some achievement, particularly as her roots were not in Guildford but in London.

Happy reading.

Nigel Enever
November 2009

Phillip Goodhand-Tait, Betty Thornton, Nigel Enever, Jim Cook and Suzanne Martin at The Sixties Exhibition, Guildford Museum 2008.

Chapter 1
Skiffle to Rock'n'Roll

Nearly everyone interviewed for this book mentioned Lonnie Donegan. *The first time I heard "Rock Island Line" is an indelible memory for me.* Lonnie was accessible. Unlike many of the American rock'n'roll artists of the late fifties, Lonnie, being British, appeared regularly on television. Not only that, his style of singing and playing was simple and therefore easily copied. Donegan was not unaware of the pivotal part he played in the development of popular music during this period. Never one to hide his light under a bushel, he even proposed the title for his autobiography to be "All Roads Lead To Lon". It is with this man that the story begins.

According to "Acts of Faith", the 1996 Adam Faith autobiography (publisher Bantam Press)

"Skiffle was a word Chris Barber and Lonnie Donegan plucked off a 1929 Paramount recording of a Rent-Party Blues session. Donegan and Barber invented their own version of this down-home black music and gave it this strange name. The whole point of skiffle was that it cost almost nothing to produce. Played on instruments knocked up out of any old thing that came to hand, skiffle music could be made by just about anyone.

"...I'd be off to 100 Oxford Street ... one evening, during the interval, on came this bloke called Lonnie Donegan. Clutching an acoustic guitar, he started singing this strange new stuff, in a raucous angry voice. By the end of the second song, that was it; I was hooked. Lonnie singing live had a fire and an anger in him that came right at you. ...

"Skiffle gave us something we'd never had before. Our own music.

1

GUILDFORD - THE ROCK'N'ROLL YEARS

The more our parents hated it, the more we revelled in it. *We don't care what Mamma don't allow, play that skiffle any old how..."*

Guildfordian Jim Cook, later of Whisker Davis, has his own take on the Lonnie Donegan phenomenon:

"I had never seen anything like Lonnie Donegan on T.V. singing "Rock Island Line". The enthusiasm and passion made the old folk song come alive. He brought to Britain his version of American folk song and blues, introducing us to Leadbelly and Woody Guthrie songs. He exported the "Rock Island Line" back to America, where it made 8 in the U.S. charts. Unfortunately, Lonnie is mostly remembered for his success with music hall type comedy songs, but by then he had inspired the next generation of music makers to learn to play the guitar.

"Also on T.V. was Tommy Steele, giving us a British version of the new American craze, rock'n'roll, an energetic off-shoot of rhythm and blues. He was also influenced by the British music hall tradition and came across as a lovable cheeky chappie.

"The Six Five Special television show for young people was a Saturday night must for me. It had a jolly youth clubby feel, but featured the new rock'n'roll."

Skiffle was a simple type of music which youngsters could easily and cheaply play. It normally involved the use of one or more acoustic guitars, a percussion instrument - probably not drums, but a washboard. The ideal was for a double bass, but often the tea chest bass was used. This comprised a tea chest with a piece of string tied to it and led up to the top of a broom handle, which was pivoted on the tea chest. The string was plucked and the handle was pulled to vary the note by changing the tension on the string. The amplification came from the transmission of the vibrations through the tea chest, producing what must have been a far from perfect pitch.

Elvis, of course, was probably more influential in his way, but less accessible. His early recordings, including the rockabilly "Baby Let's

Play House" were as exciting if not more exciting than the early Donegan recordings. Elvis was younger and more dangerous than Donegan. He had the style and the voice. In fact, he had everything, but it is back to skiffle for the moment.

♪♫

The Doolahats were a Guildford skiffle group, who got together in about 1957, with Claude Wilkins on guitar and vocals, Mick Cranham on tea chest bass, Chris Winters on guitar and Chris Arkle on washboard. In 1958 the line up changed with Johnny Kelly joining on lead guitar, Chris Arkle switching to snare drum, Les Owen playing bass, Micky Lampard on guitar and Claude Wilkins continuing as front man on vocals and guitar. Later that year Stan Newman came in on washboard.

l - r: Chris Winters, Chris Arkle, Mick Cranham and Claude Wilkins.

♪♫

GUILDFORD - THE ROCK'N'ROLL YEARS

Dave Brice has the honour of being the oldest person interviewed for this book, born right at the end of 1938 in Merrow. He was involved in three major groups in the Guildford area in the late 1950s and early sixties and could even be said to be the founding father of this type of music in this area.

Even in the early 1950s, or soon after, Dave was listening to Radio Luxembourg, which broadcast on a Saturday evening between 11 p.m. and midnight. He was inspired by the big bands and guitar music and acquired (and still retains) a large collection of 78s by bands such as Ted Heath and Johnny Dankworth, together with guitar music by Arthur "Guitar Boogie" Smith and Les Paul and even a number of early Presley recordings. He recalls attending dances promoted by Sid Norris at the T.A. Drill Hall in Artillery Terrace, featuring bands such as The Squadronaires and The Ray Ellison Quartet.

Compared with most of the characters who appear in this book, Dave was relatively late in actually starting to play music. Indeed, it was about 1957, when he was 18 years old, that he played in a skiffle group on the washboard and tea chest bass.

In the 1940s the Brice family had moved from Merrow to Bellfields and David attended Northmead School. However, he passed his 13-plus and took a place at Guildford Junior Technical School, which was part of the Technical College in Stoke Road and later, aged 15, commenced an apprenticeship with the South Eastern Electricity Board. When he reached the age of 18 he would normally have been called up for National Service, but the arrangement at that time was for those on apprenticeship to have National Service deferred. He clearly recalls National Service being abolished on 30th August, 1960 and completing his apprenticeship on 3rd September that year. He still has the letter from H.M. Government confirming that he was not required for National Service. He has hung on to this in case they decided to renege on their promise!

Dave's first week's wage as an apprentice was £1.13s.6d. By the

SKIFFLE TO ROCK'N'ROLL

age of 18 this had risen to about £4 a week, but he still needed to do a Sunday paper round to supplement his income. His paper round was run by Triggers Newsagents and took in Harts Gardens in Stoughton. By this time he had acquired a cheap acoustic guitar, which he was struggling to learn, and each week on his paper round he passed a particular house from which he heard the sounds of an expert guitarist. One day he summed up the courage to knock on the door and met the originator of the sounds, one Chris Crinnell. Chris, an Anglo-Indian, was younger than David and indeed still at school - at St. Peter's, Merrow. His father worked in Dennis Brothers. David and Chris soon became friends and with the combination of Chris's talent and Dave's record collection, the two of them developed their music to the point where they were able to form a group, which became known as The Rhythm Five.

According to David, Chris Crinnell was the best guitarist he ever played with.

"He was note perfect and pitch perfect. He could listen to a tune once and play it instantly. I don't know how he did it.

"When we formed The Rhythm Five, Chris had a small Gibson acoustic or semi-acoustic 'F' hole guitar with pick-ups. I acquired an unusual guitar, which I saw advertised in the Melody Maker. This was a solid guitar, made in Balham. In fact, as I understand it, only three such guitars were made. I had one, Joe Brown had one and I'm not sure who had the third. They were made out of old church pews!

"The line up was Chris Crinnell (lead guitar and singer), Ray West (double bass), Doug Hammond (drums), and myself on rhythm guitar. Occasionally, we had the services of a Hawaiian guitarist.

"Doug Hammond worked at Seeboard. He was quite a lot older than me and had played in dance bands for years. We were quite possibly the first group of our type in the Guildford area. Rock'n'roll was in its infancy and we played a mixture of popular tunes and mainstream easy listening type music."

GUILDFORD - THE ROCK'N'ROLL YEARS

Chris Crinnell centre stage.

The Rhythm Five only lasted about a year. Chris was keen to develop his musical career and obtain some professional work in Israel. Dave now met up with a new group of musicians who formed The Crescendos. The original line up of this group was John Kelly on lead guitar, Dave Brice on rhythm, Les Owen on bass guitar (Les graduated from the double bass), Laurie Way on drums, John Moon on piano and Tony Spencer, vocals. This group had a more rock'n'roll sound. Chris had been an excellent Chet Atkins-type of guitarist. Indeed, Dave describes him as a forerunner of Mark Knopfler. Johnny Kelly was a bit noisier on the guitar according to Dave and more suited to the type of music now becoming popular. At this stage the uniform for the group was black shirts and red ties.

Dave's contacts by now included Sid Norris, the promoter who arranged gigs at The Dorking Halls. This was probably the biggest gig in the area, until The Civic Hall arrived. The Crescendos were generally used as a well paid support group. The line up by this time

SKIFFLE TO ROCK'N'ROLL

had changed, in that three of the musicians had been replaced. There was a new bass guitarist and pianist and the drummer Laurie Way was replaced by Kenny Pate. The group also now was more commonly known as Johnny Kelly and The Rocking Crescendos.

The photograph of The Crescendos features the replacement drummer, Kenny Pate and was taken in St. Francis School, Westborough, the junior school in the old part of Southdown Avenue.

The Crescendos

It was with this line up at The Dorking Halls, supporting a group who had previously played with Hank and Bruce of The Shadows and was headed by Charlie Chester's son Peter on drums, that the latter decided to recruit those of The Rocking Crescendos that he could to turn professional. Those recruited, of course, did not include Kenny Pate as Charlie's son was the drummer. Nor could it include Dave Brice, who was still doing his apprenticeship. Mick Douglas took Dave's place. Mick's side of the story is dealt with later in this chapter.

Dave now had a year or two off music, concentrating on his

GUILDFORD - THE ROCK'N'ROLL YEARS

apprenticeship and final exams. He still continued some involvement with the music business and worked on the door at The Plaza on Saturdays and Sundays. Part of his job was to meet artists such as Gene Vincent on the outskirts of the town and escort them to the venue, including guiding them through the back door to avoid the fans. By 1961/62, however, with his apprenticeship out of the way, he decided to form his own band and this was The Kossacks (see Chapter 3).

♫♫

Another of the elder statesmen or founding fathers of the Guildford rock'n'roll movement is Mick Douglas ("Dougo"), born slightly after Dave Brice at the beginning of the 1940s. *I visited him at his home in Guildford and he showed me through to the music room, where there is a stack of memorabilia, including his vinyl collection featuring some of his own recordings, including with Adam Faith and The HiFi's.*[1] Mick is a prolific artist and his watercolours of various Guildford scenes adorn the lounge, whilst there are paintings still in progress in the music room.

The inspiration for Mick Douglas to start playing guitar in the mid fifties and pursue a career in rock'n'roll came from Bill Hayley, and in particular his film "Rock Around The Clock". Indeed, when Hayley visited England in 1956, Mick went up to see him in Kilburn, north London.

Although inspired by such as Hayley and Little Richard, Mick's first musical outing was in a skiffle group. This was in 1957 and the group was known as The Plebians. They started gigging straight away,

---

[1] The latter album is "Snakes and Hi-Fi's". Mick composed and sang some of the songs on this album and produced the cover photo.

SKIFFLE TO ROCK'N'ROLL

Mick Douglas in his studio, 2008.

the first gig being at The United Reformed Church Hall in Westborough, only a few yards from where Mick now lives.

The skiffle group was unusual in that it had a drummer rather than a washboard player and one of the drummers Mick Douglas played with around that time was John Dixon. The skiffle group only lasted a few months and Mick then turned electric.

Mick purchased his first acoustic guitar from Collis Wood in North Street, run by Mrs. Buchanan, whose son Doug also played the guitar. The cost of this guitar was the princely sum of £3.10 shillings. The first electric guitar, the Hofner Futurama, was purchased from Barnes & Avis run by Betty Sherrington (nee Thornton). Mick was a student at Farnham Art School from ages 14 to 18. His parents must have been very accommodating, as he recalls them having to take out the hire purchase on the gear.

Mick's Dad was an accomplished musician with a dance band, playing both sax and violin, and although rock'n'roll was not their scene, Mum and Dad encouraged Mick to go into the business. Amongst the venues Mick played were various coffee bars, including one in Chertsey Street where Mick says "the squaddies used to come in and beat us up - great fun!".

Around 1959 The Plaza ballroom was opened by Ken Slater. Ken Brewer was the Manager. Mick now joined a band known as The Tropics and led by Chris Crinnel. They became regulars at The Plaza. Shortly after this Mick turned pro with The Crescendos.

The full line-up of the Crescendos now included Micky Fitzpatrick from Woking on electric bass, Mick Douglas on rhythm guitar, John Kelly from Guildford on lead guitar, Claude Wilkins also from Guildford on vocals, Alan Watson on tenor sax and Pete Chester, the leader, on drums. The group became known as The Pete Chester Combo. Alan Watson was later replaced by Chris Andrews (of "Yesterday's Man" fame) on piano.

Claude Wilkins' father ran a removals business and Claude, due to the need to assist his father in the business, only lasted a few months with the band. Mick says that as for himself, he was so besotted with pop music and playing in groups that there was no question of him not going pro. The band now started touring and supporting such acts as Gene Vincent, Bert Weedon and Matt Monroe. Gigs included such prestigious venues as The London Palladium with Tommy Trinder. They were also involved in the early package tours, including The Guildford Odeon, and then the band toured Europe. On the package tours they played right through the show, backing all the solo artists.

The band made some recordings through the Roy Tempest agency, Mick receiving £13 for each recording. This was the equivalent to two week's wages for most people, and was received by each of the band members for a single recording session. They had frequent mentions in the music press, including The Melody Maker, but fame as such did not come their way.

One interesting aside is that the Pete Chester Combo was actually playing in Chippenham on the night that Eddie Cochran died in that area and Mick recalls hearing of the event the next day. Many years later, in 2006, Mick's band Razzle Dazzle played at the Eddie Cochran Memorial Concert.

The Pete Chester band toured Israel for three months. Mick, in fact, believes that they were the first band of this type to tour Israel and they played large venues there, including theatres and football stadia. For this tour, Chris Crinnell had replaced John Kelly on lead guitar. On their return from Israel, The Peter Chester Combo disbanded.

Some members of the band now got together to form Chris Revel and the Ravers. Chris Revel was in fact Chris Andrews. Micky Fitzpatrick was still with the band, but the drummer was now Norman Farrow from Walton. This new band toured Germany, mainly American forces bases. Their British gigs included support to such luminaries as The Rolling Stones. Mick says: "We supported the Stones with this band when they played at Hastings Caves. I recall having a conversation with Keith Richard and at that time he was very jealous of the success The Beatles were having."

The Beatles were also of course in Germany in the early sixties. They were contemporaries of Mick's, but at this time were just another band. On returning from Germany, The Beatles released their first single "Love Me Do" and they were no longer "just another band", although slightly later in the sixties, Mick played at The Pickwick Club in London, where all the groups hung out, and on that occasion who should be present in the audience but - you guessed it - The Beatles. Also present were The Small Faces and Goldie and the Gingerbreads. Mick, ever a ladies man, has particularly fond memories of Goldie and the Gingerbreads, but that's another book!

Next up for Mick Douglas were the Hi-Fi's, based in Germany. This band lasted from 1963 to 1967 and had two hits in Germany. Mick composed a number of the songs. Although mainly based in Germany, the Hi-Fi's returned to play in Guildford on a number of occasions and Mick finally returned permanently in the late sixties. It was around this time that Mick formed a trio with Jimmy King and Norman Farrow and a girl singer. They auditioned at The Golden Garter Club in Manchester and were accepted to be the resident band at this large cabaret club. They were there for six months and played other clubs in the Manchester area.

Mick's professional career ran from 1960 to 1976. The last professional band he was in was a trio in Devon, playing various holiday camps. By this time, at the age of 35, he thought that his image was regarded as too old for the pop scene - ironic considering that in 2008 he was still playing with Razzle Dazzle at age 67!

The former band members and their offspring are still close. For example, Pete Anderton's (see chapter 6) son married Claude Wilkins' daughter and The Crescendos reformed for the gig in June 2008, including Micky Fitzpatrick, John Kelly and with Pete Anderton on drums. On the subject of weddings, Mick was Ritchie Blackmore's (of

Deep Purple) best man and has played at various wedding receptions and at Cranleigh Village Hall with Eric Clapton. Mick met Ritchie in Germany and they have become the best of buddies over the years.

♪♪

Peter Arthur was born in January 1942 at Castle Street, in the shadow of the castle keep and the old indoor swimming pool. The two-up, two-down cottage with outdoor toilet has long since been demolished. He attended Holy Trinity primary school and Pewley secondary. At age 15 Peter left school and became one of the many Guildford musicians interviewed to join a gents outfitters - in this case, Hepworths - why gents outfitters? Good-looking and personable young men, no doubt. At Hepworths Peter in his words "had to wear a proper suit - not a teddy boy drape jacket - the teddy boy era was in any event fading out at this stage."

Peter's first venture into music was, of course, a skiffle group. In this case, he played washboard and his brother, David, a tea chest bass. The group also featured an electric guitarist and a drummer by the name of Bert Curtis (later of The Age Beaters). They all sang, although in Peter's words the sound was "not particularly good". They appear to have been relatively sophisticated of their type though, with their uniform of white shirts with black spots, giving rise to the group's name The Leopard Spots. They also entered a competition for a show to be known as the "Six Five Special Show" at the Guildford Odeon in 1958. Apart from Lonnie Donegan, influences at this time included The Vipers skiffle group and Chas McDevitt.

When this group folded after about six months, Peter found himself going along to see various groups at The Plaza Ballroom, one of whom was Johnny Kidd and The Pirates. On one occasion, when The Pirates were playing without Johnny Kidd, there was a talent competition where members of the audience were asked to come up and sing with The Pirates. Peter volunteered himself to sing one of Johnny's songs, won the competition and was spotted by a member of The Rhythmics, who asked if he would like to join them as vocalist.

The Rhythmics' first gig was at The Plaza. Even for a one-off gig there was a contract. The performance was to take place on 18th November, 1960, and the salary was to be £4. Details of the contract include the fact that "all persons accompanying the group, apart from the agent, are to pay full admission price" and "no tuning to be allowed on stage once the show has commenced". There was also the draconian clause that "should the artistes fail to appear without just cause, the company may hold them liable by way of damages in the sum of £50".

The group's line-up comprised Tom O'Looney and Chris Butcher on guitars, Jeff Salmon on drums, Ted Castle on bass (later to be replaced by Errol Newman) and vocalist Peter. They were all from Guildford, apart from Errol who hailed from Woking. They also later acquired a female vocalist, Penny Collins, from Aldershot.

The Rhythmics with Penny Collins

The photograph below shows left to right Tom O'Looney, Chris Butcher, Peter Arthur, Jeff Salmon and Errol Newman.

Peter's middle name was Richard and hence the stage name Ricky. The name Clayton was chosen at random.

The Rhythmics never achieved their aim of becoming professional, but at one time in the early sixties were known as Guildford's top group, or even as one Surrey Advertiser headline would have it "Surrey's top group". There was a report in The Surrey Advertiser of a charity concert, organised by the Guildford School of Arts Students' Union at The Civic Hall in November 1963 with music by "Humphrey Lyttelton, Cyril Davies All Stars with Long John Baldry, and two local groups, The Rhythmics and The Yard Birds". Note the spelling of The Yardbirds, their reference to being local and their billing below The Rhythmics. Also around this period there is a reference in The Surrey Advertiser to "the favourite local groups" as being respectively Phill and The Stormsville Shakers, Ricky Clayton and The Rhythmics and The Age Beaters.

GUILDFORD - THE ROCK'N'ROLL YEARS

Ricky and The Rhythmics on top of the world - well, The Tunsgate Club anyway.

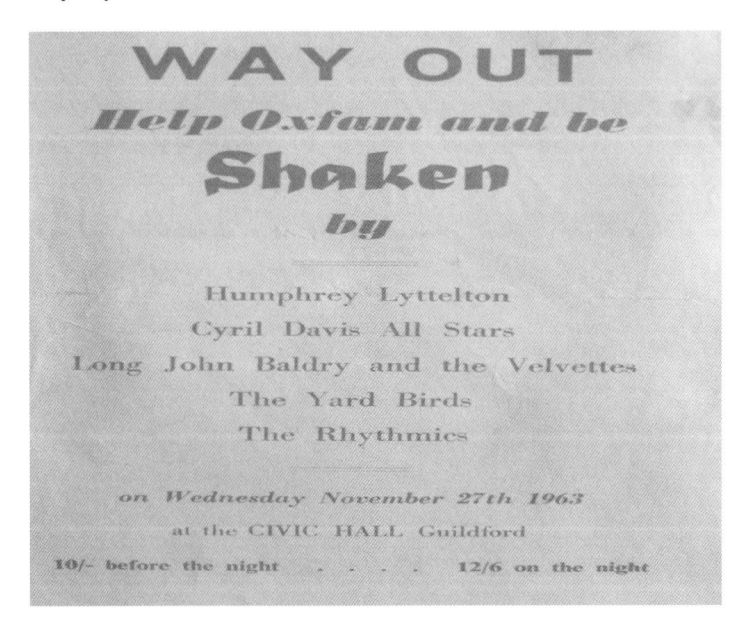

WAY OUT

Help Oxfam and be

Shaken

by

Humphrey Lyttelton
Cyril Davis All Stars
Long John Baldry and the Velvettes
The Yard Birds
The Rhythmics

on Wednesday November 27th 1963
at the CIVIC HALL Guildford

10/- before the night .... 12/6 on the night

Other gigs included Club Butaca in Old Woking and, of course, The Tunsgate Club. A picture of Ricky and The Rhythmics on the roof of The Tunsgate Club appeared in The Surrey Advertiser under the caption "Ricky and The Rhythmics reach the top". There is a further picture of Ricky in his stage suit, so admired by Billy Fury that he acquired one of his own! The suit was, in Ricky's words, "a grey silvery suit" which he had designed in Guildford. The story behind the Billy Fury incident was that whilst with The Rhythmics, Ricky was endeavouring to obtain a solo professional contract and was auditioned by Larry Parnes. Parnes wanted Ricky to sign a contract, one of the terms of which was "no steady girlfriends". As Ricky was engaged at this time his signature was not forthcoming. This was at a time when Billy Fury had yet to be established. Larry had already chosen Ricky's name - "Johnny Dove" - to go along with the likes of Fury, Marty Wild and Vince Eager. In what will become a familiar theme in this book, Peter exchanged his semi-professional musical career for the stability and security of married life. The power of managers and agents and the stark choices facing young artistes seem incredibly alien in today's flexible world.

Chapter 2
The Cranleigh and Godalming Connections

There cannot be many Guildfordians who do not have a link with Cranleigh through friends or relatives. The village has expanded over the years, although even in the sixties it claimed to be the largest in England. It is perhaps best known for its school and cricket green and, to some extent in those days, the old cinema and village hall. Pre Beeching, it was of course linked by rail to Guildford and Horsham, providing a ready means of transport for the inhabitants of the nearby villages and hamlets, including Bramley and Shamley Green. However, in the context of this book, the best known thing about Cranleigh in the sixties was The Bumblies.

Like Dougo of the previous chapter, Terry Ward was an arts school product, as were such rock luminaries as John Lennon, Ronnie Wood, Ray Davis, Jeff Beck, Jimmy Page, Charlie Watts, Keith Richards and Pete Townshend, to name but a few! Again, like Dougo, Terry appears to have transferred to art school at an early stage in his school career and it was here that he firmed up his friendship with the future Bumblies drummer, Richard Hodby.

It was Terry's view that the art schools were so prolific in producing rock musicians, because there was too little else to do at college. There was no compulsion to attend lectures. We just "brought in our guitars to practice and fill in the time". Whilst this may be partly true, there is no doubt also that the Bohemian and artistic temperament was attracted towards the new musical fashions.

Terry Ward's parents were evacuated from Dulwich during the war and settled in Cranleigh. David Terence Ward was born in Mount Alvernia Nursing Home, Harvey Road, Guildford in 1943.

THE CRANLEIGH AND GODALMING CONNECTIONS

Terry's first education was at a prep school in Cranleigh, but from age 8 to 15 at St. Peter's Catholic private school in Merrow run by priests. Terry commuted from Cranleigh to Merrow on a daily basis as a day boy. He jokes that it was his mother's way of keeping him in order, the alternative being to board, the boarding part of the school being likened to the Stalag prisoner of war camp! Says Terry: "Pupils were caned for having one blazer button undone!". He admits to not being particularly academically minded and left there before taking GCEs to attend Guildford Art School for two years.

There is music in Terry's family history. His grandfather, who was blind from the age of 21, was a piano tuner, busked on Blackpool beach and played for the silent movies. One of Terry's uncles sang opera and the other played double bass with such dance band greats as Edmundo Ross, Ted Heath and Billy Cotton.

It was around 1956 that Terry first heard Lonnie Donegan and also saw a skiffle group on a lorry at the Cranleigh carnival, performing Johnny Duncan's "Last Train to San Fernando". This was another of those life-changing moments and Terry decided that this was what he wanted to do.

He therefore went about forming a small skiffle group. He and his mates played in the garage of his house, which opened onto the street, and the passers-by were entertained with free concerts! He practised assiduously, listening over and over again to his Dansette record player to the tracks to be learnt.

By 1958 he had moved on to art college and therefore had more time to pursue his musical career[1]. In 1959 The Senators were formed

---

[1] Author's note: Guildford School of Art was a separate entity to the Tech, but shared the same building. In my first term at the Tech in 1963, there was an R & B Club at the Art School. It was here that I first heard The Rolling Stones with their first record, Chuck Berry's "C'mon".

GUILDFORD - THE ROCK'N'ROLL YEARS

Terry looking rather startled with hero Bill Hayley.

with John Dixon on lead guitar, Ray (the window cleaner from Guildford) on double bass, Richard Hodby on snare drum with brushes, Terry on vocals, and for part of the time included Mick Douglas. This group entered one of the many competitions held at The Plaza Ballroom in Guildford for local bands from the Surrey area. The winners were Tony Crowe and The Counts, from Woking. The Senators came last, after which, according to Terry "we went into hiding for a while".

At 16 Terry took part in an audition for a television show in Southampton and with The Senators played at the art school college party at The Stoke Hotel in support to Acker Bilk.

"Trad jazz was all the rage. There were the trad jazzers and the rockers, two totally different camps, and we didn't always see eye to eye. I was a bit of a rocker. We went to school in plastic jackets, hoping that one day we'd be able to afford the real thing! The jazzers were the long pullovers, corduroys and sandals types with beards. They went to Boxers Coffee Bar in Guildford and we used to go to

THE CRANLEIGH AND GODALMING CONNECTIONS

Mac's Café at the top of North Street, run by Mr. and Mrs. De Vito. This was where the local rockers hung out in those days.

"I did a washing up job there in the art school holidays and got to know the local motorcycling fraternity.

"I was asked to leave the art school and then started work at Dunn & Co., the hatters, in Guildford - not my scene.

"Then I went off to work as a red coat for Butlins. I remember I went up to Oxford with my brother for an audition. I did an Elvis Presley song and they said "right, you're an entertaining red coat" - this meant I was paid £7 a week instead of £5. I went to Pwllheli in North Wales. This was at the age of 18. The resident rock band there was Rory Storm and The Hurricanes, with drummer Ringo Starr. I occasionally sang with them."

One of Terry's early managers, Tony Pleasance, liked to bill Terry in his early days as "Shaking Terry Maine, the Columbia sensational recording star". To most the name "Maine" would not appear any more sensational than the name "Ward", except possibly the connotation with the lion's mane. By Terry's own admission, he had never been near a recording studio. Under this name he played at a few local village halls as a feature singer for other bands. From time to time in his career Terry was also billed as Terry "Shaker" Ward.

Another of Terry's early inspirations was Chris Crinnel (who had been in Terry's year at St. Peter's) performing with The Tropics at The Plaza. Terry distinctly remembers Chris's version of "Mean Streak" and that The Tropics were limited to a three piece with no drummer, but with an electric solid upright bass and Dougo on rhythm guitar.

It was after this that John Terry and The Mustangs were formed, the name deriving from the two lead singers, John Cooper and Terry Ward. This line up included Mick Clark on bass (later to form The Bumblies), Anthony Hawks on lead guitar and Howard Dixon (the brother of John Dixon) on rhythm guitar. The idea of two vocalists

21

was unusual but not unique. Indeed, The Nashville Teens followed this format and Terry says "with the same usual ego problems".

Following success with The Mustangs, Terry Ward and his cohorts (mainly from Cranleigh) formed The Bumblies. They stuck to the two vocalists format (although the band was shortly to reduce to Terry as the sole vocalist) and the line up was Maurice Shelly (vocals), Terry Ward (vocals), Godfrey ("Goff") Matthews (pianist), Tony ("Ant") Hawks (lead guitarist), Mick Clark (bass guitar) and Richard Hodby (drums).

Goff in his website describes them as a harmony band in the style of The Moody Blues. Terry's description was pop rather than R & B. Various snippets of information can be gleaned about The Bumblies, in particular from an article in The Surrey Advertiser towards the end of 1964. For example, a description of their distinctive stage outfits made of "crombie, with velvet trimmings".

The Surrey Advertiser in July 1964 indicates the band to be one of the Guildford "Big Three". This is an intriguing description and does not indicate which other two bands were considered to be part of the Big Three - The Stormsville Shakers presumably, The Age Beaters possibly? In any event, the article indicates that The Bumblies were the first local group to have an official fan club set up in the Guildford area. This was set up by Jackie Keevill, with the co-operation of the group's manager, Bruce Bunker.

By this stage the group was playing throughout Surrey and parts of Hampshire and on average had about four dates a week. Prestige dates included The 2 I's Coffee Bar in Soho and The Kingston Jazz Cellar, but also many less prestigious venues, including various village halls, venues in Aldershot and The Sandfield Terrace Ballroom. They also performed at a lot of private parties and made a regular appearance at The Tunsgate Club. The gig fees were more than handy. According to Terry

"My typical income from gigs exceeded what I was earning in my

THE 'BUMBLIES'

Management:
B. J. BUNKER
19 Addison Road, Guildford
Telephone 62726

Fan Club:
MISS L. BUNKER
19 Addison Road, Guildford
Telephone 62726

The Bumblies with the two vocalists 1964.
Back row l - r: Tony (Ant) Hawkes, Godfrey (Goff) Matthews, and Mick Clarke
Middle row : Richard Hodby
Front row l-r: Maurice Shelley and Terry Ward.

day job in a car dealership. The one gig for which we had to work for much less than normal was The Tunsgate Club, which only paid £6. At one point our manager tried to negotiate a raise to £7. We considered calling in Alan Klein to sort it out! After protracted discussions, Tom Stredwick would not agree to a raise of £7 and as a result we did not appear at the club for some months. Eventually, however, we missed the gig too much and agreed to return. I think a compromise was reached at £6.10s, plus a free half of lager and lime - quite an exotic drink in those days!

"Ant's best guitar was a Gibson Stereo. Prior to that he had a Fenton Weill. The Gibson guitar was similar to that used by Joe Brown. It was the most expensive guitar on the market at the time and cost £260, an enormous sum for those days."

Terry recalls being able to park outside The Harvest Moon Club and even park in Wardour Street when playing at The Flamingo. Getting to London, however, was in some ways not so easy. The advent of the new A3 and the M25 in the 1970s and 80s dramatically reduced the journey time to parts of London. Looking at old photos of Guildford, or indeed any town in the fifties and sixties, one thing stands out - the lack of cars. Readers of a certain age will indeed remember being able to park in the High Street without hindrance.

Terry also remembers the manager of the famous 2 I's coffee bar, Tom Littlewood, being a crafty so-and-so, who advertised to audition bands for work in Germany. As it turns out he had no contacts whatsoever in Germany, but numerous bands turned up for the so-called auditions, providing him with free entertainers.

THE CRANLEIGH AND GODALMING CONNECTIONS

There was one amusing incident at The Central Ballroom, Aldershot. The Bumblies turned up as the support group to The Moody Blues. At this stage The Moody Blues had not yet arrived. The manager assumed that The Bumblies were, in fact, The Moody Blues and they decided not to correct this misapprehension. They were shown round the premises in some detail, including the hospitality suite where there were free drinks for the "celebrities". The manager's final instructions to them were "right lads, at the end of the show don't hang about, we gotta get you out of here quickly" and at this moment the real Moody Blues turned up! One cannot imagine that the manager was best pleased, although The Bumblies had never said that they were anyone other than themselves.

A favourite type of gig was the posh private party at one of the local large houses. At one private party, run by a couple of Arabs, the wine was not exactly flowing, so the group got them all to do the Conga. They conga'd in a long line out to the garden and says Terry "when they were half way round the rose bed we purloined one of the crates of wine which were stacked up behind the band".

In 1964 the band was renamed Terry Ward and The Bumblies and was joined by Jonathan King (then known as Kenneth King), who negotiated for them a record contract with Fontana. Kenneth wrote the song "Gotta Tell" for the band and this was released in 1965. This song was backed with "When I Come To You". Also according to Goff's website "many hours were then spent recording with Joe Meek, well known for his production of such favourites as "Telstar", only for the project to come to an abrupt halt following Meek's sudden death".

The background to Kenneth's interest in The Bumblies derives from the fact that he lived at Ewhurst. One day he called at Terry's house, said that he understood that Terry had a band and indicated that he wished to become involved.

Kenneth began a partial role as a manager for the group, but also wanted to gain experience as a singer by doing a few numbers per gig with The Bumblies as his backing group. Kenneth brought along his own soap box to stand on and purchased some ladies boots from Dolcis, which came up to his knees. This did not do the band's street cred any good at all! Perhaps the most bizarre episode is best described in Terry's own words.

"Kenneth actually talked me into going up to Regents Park Zoo in his little Austin Healy Sprite and buying a monkey, which we then brought back from Regents Park to Cranleigh and he lived in a cage in my house. We did a gig at The Civic Hall with the monkey on my shoulder. The monkey's name was George, but after a few weeks things were getting too strenuous and he could not be controlled. He was certainly not toilet trained. He was a lovely little animal, but he had to go!"

Despite Kenneth's advice to stay in England and keep making records as the key to success, The Bumblies were desperate to travel overseas. In retrospect, Terry admits that of course Kenneth was right. Kenneth wanted them to record "Detroit City" by Bobby Bear. More significantly, Kenneth had plans to give The Bumblies the song

THE CRANLEIGH AND GODALMING CONNECTIONS

"Good News Week", which in the event went to Hedgehogs Anonymous, who had a hit with this. As Terry recalls, however, "they were a novice band, who had one tour which fell flat, but they had had the hit - albeit as one-hit-wonders".

Kenneth had now come up with a song for himself, which was "Everyone's Gone To The Moon". Ant worked out the chords with him and did the demo, but did not appear on the final recording. The rest of the Jonathan King story is history, not all of it good.

Around this time there were some setbacks for The Bumblies, including the loss of their van and their manager, and the illness of the lead guitarist, but their number of gigs appeared to be on the increase, including regular appearances at The Civic Hall, with Dave Everson of The Age Beaters stepping in as lead guitarist, during Ant's temporary incapacity.

Terry was very keen to turn professional. Some of the parents of band members were not so keen. It was a very big gamble. The age of majority was then 21 and below that age parents technically had control. Ant had a good job with the insurance company, Commercial Union. Richard also had a good job in the world of commercial art.

In October 1966 Terry finally acted unilaterally on his ambitions to turn pro when he saw an advertisement in The Melody Maker for a singer. It transpired the band advertising was The Shindigs from Leicester, whose current vocalist was Jerry Dorsey. This particular singer, born Arnold George Dorsey, did not see eye to eye with the band, changed his name to Englebert Humperdink, and went on to great things as a solo performer.

The Shindigs came down to Cranleigh, took lodgings, worked in the local garden centre and rehearsed in the evening. Terry and The Shindigs then took themselves off to Germany to play the U.S. army bases. Terry recalls "It was not very pleasant. We were all in one room. One band member, who shall remain nameless, never changed his socks and shoes! There were problems with the police."

GUILDFORD - THE ROCK'N'ROLL YEARS

Terry's girlfriend of the time was Ann Blake, known as "Tosca"[1]. She had been a fellow student with him at Guildford Art College. She joined him on this tour as a singer. As Terry says: "You had to have a girl singer on the tours of the American bases. It did not matter if she could not sing, as long as she looked good."

Whilst Terry was away The Bumblies carried on rehearsing and they kept in contact, particularly Terry and Richard Hodby, with whom Terry had been at art school. On his return to England, The Bumblies re-formed and Terry answered another advertisement in The Melody Maker, this time from the Claydon Agency in Aldgate, London. He went up there and what could be described as The Bumblies' French connection was established.

The band as a whole finally decided to go professional at around the end of 1966/the beginning of 1967, now as a five piece with Terry Ward, Richard Hodby and Goff brought forward from the previous Bumblies, to be joined by Peter Mould on bass guitar and Roger Giffin on lead guitar. The band toured France with great success at such leading venues as Paris's St. Hilaire Club, although their first gig was near Rouen. They made further contacts in the Rouen area, which enabled them to tour France in their Ford transit and the itinerary took in Paris and Orange.

A typical gig would be in a marquee, which was set up on the Saturday and according to Terry "The peasants used to come in from the surrounding villages. Having been bored out of their minds all week, they proceeded to get drunk and start a fight. On one occasion, someone fired a shotgun into the ceiling. Back in England, things were not so extreme, although there were rivalries between villages

---

[1] Tosca was a good friend of The Bumblies and also friends with Jerry and John Neve, who ran The Harvest Moon. It was she who painted the black and white mural scenes, which adorned the walls of that particular venue.

THE CRANLEIGH AND GODALMING CONNECTIONS

The Bumblies in France, June 1967. l - r: Terry Ward (vocals), Peter Mould (bass), Roger Giffin (lead guitar), Godfrey Matthews (keyboard) and Richard Hodby (drums).

and punch-ups were not uncommon, particularly at the ABC dances which were held in various village halls."

In the early days Godfrey played the stand-up piano with a microphone inside connected to the PA system. Virtually all venues had a piano in those days, but whether or not it would be in tune was another matter. A much better arrangement was the use of the electronic keyboards, although this was early days for this type of instrument. The Farfisa organ was in common use, but Godfrey chose a Hohner pianette, purchased from Barnes & Avis, for his tour of France.

As to rivalry between bands, this was not a particular feature in Terry's opinion, although there was a certain amount of musical snobbery.

"The Stormsville Shakers took themselves very seriously. We used to lark around on stage. By and large though, all the bands got on very well. For example, I used to go and watch The Primevals at The

Tunsgate Club. I enjoyed the energy in their music."

Terry was professional altogether from 1966 to 1978 and his last professional booking was a residency at The Hammersmith Palais with The Tony Evans Band, a 14-piece band of the Joe Loss type who had performed on Come Dancing. In common with most of his contemporaries on the sixties rock scene, Terry has continued his musical career on a semi-pro basis, virtually until the present day.

♪♫

In Guildford circles, Dick Middleton is a bit of a legend. Born in 1942, Richard, like Terry Ward, was a pupil at St. Peter's School in Merrow.

His introduction to rock'n'roll was in the school gym, where he heard for the first time Gene Vincent's "Be Bop A Lula".

"I heard this incredible sound - the guitar solo by Cliff Gallop - little did I think that within five years I would be playing that solo alongside Gene Vincent.

"We formed a skiffle group, which included Chris Crinell (see chapter 1) and myself on drums. I later moved over to the guitar and the line up developed to include Terence Hutchins on bass and Peter Hawkins on drums. I used to practise every day. I had an acoustic guitar with a horrible action. I used to go to bed with that guitar. I even slept with it outside in the summer, but it did not have a truss rod and as a result the neck warped!"

Dick graduated from his acoustic with the horrible action to an F-hole Hofner with a pick up, but the great step up came when his dad took him up to Shaftesbury Avenue and bought him a Gibson Les Paul Junior for 68 guineas and a Gibson valve amp with a 10" speaker.

"But what a great sound. My father was a dentist and not particularly into music, but I guess we must have been reasonably well off for him to have made these acquisitions on my behalf. For me there was now no looking back. I only wanted to listen to American guitarists and, in particular, The Ventures.

Dick Middleton still rocking, 2008, Angmering.

"I now formed a group called The Seekers. The line up of this group was Peter Clifton (vocals and guitar), Terence Hutchins (bass), Peter Hawkins (drums) and myself on lead guitar."

His parents were supportive in that dad used to drive them in the van and mum let them practise at her school. She had a prep school, Fernlea, in Busbridge Lane, Godalming. A number of other local musicians used to rehearse there, including Kirk Riddle and Graham "Cupcake" Cooper. Dick went to piano lessons with Dave Sherrington (later of The Stormsville Shakers alongside Kirk Riddle), "just to learn the rudiments of music".

Ivor Shackleton (later also of The Stormsville Shakers) remembers walking home from Godalming Grammar School and hearing what sounded like a very professional guitarist practising who was, in fact, Dick. A little later on Ivor was round at Dick's house and remembers him demonstrating some of his Chet Atkins style of play. "Great stuff". Much later after Ivor had left The Shakers and was playing bass, he was with Dick in a band called "Ram".

Dick played in The Peppermint Lounge in the basement, a coffee bar in Chertsey Street, Guildford.

"Because I could play all the rock'n'roll licks, the teds wanted me to play there. I was probably about 18, but looked about 14, and there I was with my Les Paul Junior and little Gibson amp, dressed up by my mum in my cavalry twills, desert boots and a tweed jacket, playing for these teds!"

The Seekers played at The Plaza on a regular basis. Other bands playing there at that time included Neil Christian and The Crusaders, whose members at various times included Jimmy Page, Albert Lee and later Dick himself.

There is a report in The Surrey Advertiser regarding the semi-final of the Red Cross Rock Contest (see next chapter) regarding Barry Stafford and The Seekers, who came third out of five contestants, which reads as follows.

"The Seekers were unlucky from the start. Twice in their first two numbers the amplifier for Richard Middleton's lead guitar packed up and in the end it was The Stormsville Shakers who came to the rescue. Richard, who went on to prove himself the most accomplished guitarist present, accepted a sporting offer from his opposite number with The Shakers and borrowed Ivor Shackleton's amplifier."

At age 19 Dick was working in Sound City in London. A number of rock artists used the shop.

THE CRANLEIGH AND GODALMING CONNECTIONS

"Keith Moon used to come in. One day he brought his mate, Pete Townshend. I showed him how to hold his first chord, D."

Dick was demonstrating guitars there when one John Lawson happened to be present and heard him playing. Lawson turned out to be Gene Vincent's bass guitarist and impressed by what he heard of Dick, asked if he was interested in working with Gene. Because of the Musicians' Union's rules, Gene could not bring over his American band. Dick could play the Cliff Gallop type licks and Gene formed his U.K. Blue Caps.

"You can imagine what it was like for me, a young guy, picking up a rock'n'roll hero from his house for a gig. We all travelled in a Commer van. We played the Liverpool Empire, De Montfort Hall, Leicester, places like that and a lot of smaller clubs."

The Surrey Advertiser reported Richard's latest venture in the following terms.

"Local guitar group, The Seekers, have lost their leader, Richard Middleton, of Busbridge Lane, Godalming. He has started a tour with American singer Gene Vincent's group and has a two to three year contract (in fact Richard recalls the contract only lasting about one year) as the lead guitarist … guitar playing is not Richard's only interest. He is also a keen footballer and is a member of the St. Peter's School (Merrow) Old Boys' Team."

Says Richard:

"When we played at The Guildford Civic Hall with Gene, our amplification would sound very primitive by today's standards. We each had an AC30. The PA was a 50 watt Vortexian amp with two 4 x 10 columns. Nothing was miked up. The only mike was for Gene. But the sound was great. The light and shade came from the band rather than any control desk."

Gene Vincent's Manager, Don Arden, thought that the U.K. Blue Caps could be a beat group like The Beatles, so the group then went out on their own under the name of Bobby Shaftoe and The Roof

GUILDFORD - THE ROCK'N'ROLL YEARS

Dick, far left, in the Gene Vincent days.

Raisers. Dick recalls their bass guitarist, John Lawson, being unbelievably good looking and them being thrown off the Little Richard tour because the crowds were stilling yelling for John when Richard came on. Brian Epstein came along to see The Roof Raisers at The Red Lion in Leytonstone and took rather a fancy to John Lawson. "John wasn't that way inclined and we heard no more." [1]

Dick Middleton was a great fan of the Ricky Nelson guitarist, James Burton, and with the aid of his Telecaster developed this type of sound. While working at Sound City, Dick met many great guitarists, including session musician Big Jim Sullivan. "I was always asking questions and learning".

Johnny Hallyday came to England from France in about 1964 to find a rhythm section. There were lots of guitarists auditioning,

---

[1] The Hard Rock Café in Las Vegas has a poster on the wall featuring Little Richard, Duane Eddie and The Roof Raisers.

THE CRANLEIGH AND GODALMING CONNECTIONS

including Eric Clapton and John McLaughlin, but they weren't what Hallyday wanted. Hallyday wanted the James Burton sound and accordingly he chose Richard.

"Hallyday was the best gig I ever had. I had no idea that he was so big in Europe. We were each paid £14 a day. We toured for a month to crowds of 20,000 and more. It was incredible. In England we did the Royal Variety Performance and Ready, Steady, Go."

The Roof Raisers were on the Don Arden tours with such as the late Gene Pitney, The Kinks and The Shirells. Dick particularly remembers when he was playing his green Gretsch and Duane Eddy was on the bill at The Fairfield Hall in Croydon, receiving the compliment from Duane "that's a real fine sound you got there, son."

Also on the bill were Gerry Marsden and The Pacemakers. When they played the Liverpool Empire, they stayed at Gerry's mum's place. Dick slept in the bath and the next morning Mrs. Marsden cooked them all egg and bacon.

After working with Hallyday and doing some session work in France, Dick returned to England in the late sixties and formed a group with some local musicians, including Jeff Beck's ex-bass guitarist, Laurie Munn on drums and Bill Enticknap on vocals. Bill had a bit of a Joe Cocker voice. He became mainly a folk singer and continues on to the present day. At that time gigs included local pubs and clubs, including The Old Manor at Farncombe.

After a semi-pro period, Dick was offered a job with Hurricane. Their producer, Barry Murray, was also Mungo Jerry's producer and asked if Dick would like to join Mungo. This was in the early seventies. Dick says

"I was nearly 30 then and yes it was great fun. I recorded with Mungo on "Alright, Alright, Alright" and "Long Legged Woman". Dick says "I was amazed how Top of the Pops worked. Arrive at 9 a.m. and there all day just to mime ….. although Ray Dorset did sing live. When we did "Long Legged Woman Dressed In Black" there was an unheard of band on that asked for my autograph ... ABBA! They were doing the Eurovision Song Contest!"

Dick (Richard) Middleton in the Mungo Jerry days.

In the seventies Dick was in the Famous Rondini Brothers, which included Dave Bidwell, the Mungo Jerry drummer, and Tony Leach of Guildford, a singer-songwriter and keyboard player of some note on the seventies Guildford music scene.

Dick spent some time in the States, where his next door neighbour was Ali McGraw. However, he says he never made much money from music, although he has earnt a living from it for most of his life. Between 1977 and '84 he ran the Dick Middleton Music Shop in Quarry Street, Guildford, next to The Kings Head.

A niche market album called "Who Invited Them?", released in 1978 on the Thumb label, features a number of the local musicians of the period, including Tony Backhurst, Chris Braine (another one time member of the Mungo Jerry band), Graham Cooper, Doug Ferguson (Camel), members of the Famous Rondini Brothers, including Tony Leach and Richard Middleton, Jackie Lynton, Stuart Reffold, Kirk Riddle and Dave Sherrington. Also during this period from 1977 to '81, Dick ran a musicians football eleven, which featured such as "animal" Roy Higgs, Dave Ramsey (drummer of The Love Affair), Doug Ferguson, et al. Around 1980 Eric Clapton played at The Royal Hotel, Stoughton, with Kirk Riddle on bass and support band headed by Dick Middleton.

Now in his late sixties, Dick is still plying his trade in gigs mainly based around his new home in Angmering, West Sussex. He can still craft a mean solo out of his classic Telecaster and Peavey valve amp. In fact, things have turned virtually full circle for Dick, with him playing again with his old mate Peter Clifton, mainly based in the Chichester area. This band, Tail Lights, played recently at the polo ground near Cranleigh run by the former Faces drummer, Kenney Jones.

Chapter 3
Kossacks and Shakers

Dave Brice was essentially a businessman. By the early sixties he had a number of contacts in the music business in the Guildford area and he decided to recruit musicians who would provide him with local commercial success, playing a wide variety of music. He himself could not sing and, by his own admission, was not the greatest of guitarists. He had another trick up his musical sleeve, however, in that he had been taught to play the drums by Kenny Pate of The Crescendos and would occasionally give Kenny a break in gigs by taking over on the skins. Kenny had been an RAF bandsman and was in Dave's words "a proper drummer".

There appeared to be plenty of guitarists available, but not many drummers. Dave therefore took up the drum slot in the new band , The Kossacks, and recruited two guitarists and a bass player, all of whom could sing, and the coup-de-grâce, the vocalist, 16-year- old Caroline Harms. Apart from Caroline and David, the other members of the band were now Radley Walker (lead guitar), Colin Tutton (rhythm guitar and piano), and David Scott (bass guitar), all vocalists. The addition of the attractive female vocalist gave the band more interest than the other all-male local bands, both from a male and female perspective.

Dave's contacts included Sid Norris (his cousin at The Plaza), Tom Stredwick, who had been a van driver at Seeboard when Dave was an apprentice and now ran The Tunsgate Club, and finally a promoter from Merrow who set up the gigs and hired the venues and split the takings with Dave's band.

According to The Guildford & Godalming Times of 12th January,

KOSSACKS AND SHAKERS

1963, The Kossacks had only been formed for about two months. This article describes The Kossacks as a group with a difference, the difference being

"A 16-year-old bundle of bounce and vitality named Caroline. The group are almost up to professional standard. I formed this opinion after hearing them at The Jubilee Club. But the boys - Dave Brice of Bellfields Estate, David "Scotty" Shaw of Wood Street, Radley Walker of Hillview Crescent, and Colin Tutton of Cobham - have no wish to turn professional, because they all have very good jobs. But Caroline Harms of Ash would give almost anything to make singing her career. She has potential - a sweet voice, good looks and a pleasant personality, together with an individual style. All Caroline needs is that lucky break."

Caroline and The Kossacks

The story behind the discovery of Caroline is that the lead guitarist, Radley, worked at the Tax Office in Leapale Lane and a friend of his, Gloria, had a friend, Caroline, who could sing. She was invited along to The Plaza for rehearsal on a Sunday morning and had no problems in convincing them that she was up to the job. Dave says:

"I had to swear to her Dad on a stack of Bibles that I would look after her and protect her from the evils of the rock'n'roll world!

"We also rehearsed at the casino above The Tunsgate Club in return for Sunday night gigs at a nominal fee."

Dave's experience and contacts led to a variety of gigs - village halls, weddings, etc. The Kossacks had such a good following that on one occasion the police had to be called to Merrow Village Hall to keep order when there was a full house and punters queuing and unable to get in. Dave's future wife, Jean, worked in a typing pool at Seeboard. He remembers causing some amusement when asking the girls to type up the words to songs for him to subsequently insert the guitar chords - with words like "Do Wah Diddy Diddy", one can understand the amusement.

A tape recording of The Kossacks in rehearsal survives and includes two guitar instrumentals. Part of the guitar sounds interesting for use of the foot volume control as a pre-cursor to the wah-wah type of sound. The one vocal track is The Springfields "Island of Dreams" and the harmonies are certainly there.

♪♪

Phillip Goodhand-Tait was born in Hull in 1945. *I had always assumed that the first part of the hyphenated double-barrelled name was a stage name reference to his abilities on the ivories!* In fact, it is the product of a complicated little bit of family history, whereby his grandparents who were Taits had adopted children from within the family by the name of Goodhand and, already having children by the name of Tait, decided that it would simplify matters all round if all the children were known as Goodhand-Taits. The change was made by Deed Poll on 8th April, 1941, so that Phill was born Goodhand-Tait,

KOSSACKS AND SHAKERS

and a very fortuitous name it has turned out to be.

Phill comes from a socialist background, his father having been an active trade unionist and actually employed at that time by the Transport and General Workers' Union. However, by the mid-1950s he, and many others like him, had decided they would seek better prospects in the more prosperous south of the country. Although it took some time, he was able to engineer a council house exchange, which ended up with him and his family moving to 20 Four Acres, Bushy Hill, Merrow, in 1957. Phill was 12 years old and his father found work at the commercial vehicle manufacturers Dennis Bros.

Phill had been in a technical school in Hull and passed his 11-plus and now continued his school career at Pewley School in Sydenham Road (later moving to George Abbot). He recalls the discipline being much softer in the south than in the north. For example, when he raised his hand to answer a question, he stood to speak. His fellow pupils found it hilarious that (a) he would feel it necessary to stand up to speak and (b) that he spoke in this strange northern accent. The latter led him to be given the nickname of ... surprise, surprise ... "Yorkshire".

Phill's mother, a graduate in music and a piano teacher, was his initial piano tutor. She taught him piano from the age of five. Although the family background was classical music, Phill was able to hear more jazz or pop orientated sounds through the medium of the radio - no T.V. and could not afford records at this time. A particular influence was Winifred Attwell (from Trinidad) and "The Black and White Rag". On the singing front his main influence was Tommy Steele with "Singing The Blues". American artists such as Jerry Lee Lewis did not enter into the equation at this stage. This type of American artist was not reaching the average English home.

The typical household accommodation arrangement in those days included two reception rooms, the rear for everyday use and the front for best, only used for visitors to have a cup of tea. However, the

41

GUILDFORD - THE ROCK'N'ROLL YEARS

piano was in the front room and accordingly Phill was therefore given the opportunity of uninterrupted practice - not however quite uninterrupted, as other kids would look through the window to watch and to some extent hear the performance - Phill's first taste of providing musical entertainment!

In Guildford Phill found a great piano teacher in Frank Winslade and he proceeded to pass all his classical theory and practical exams - a fact he was later to keep quiet about when forming The Stormsville Shakers! - perhaps partly through it not being then thought cool to be associated with classical music, but also in part because he wanted to be a singer and not a pianist.

There is an early picture of Phill (taken at Burpham Village Hall, c. 1960/61) in the prototype rock'n'roll group known as The Royphillians, with two acoustic guitarists, a vocalist and Phill on the piano. The guitarists could not play normal chords and had to tune their guitars so that the open strings formed a chord! The singer (not Phill at this stage) was the class heart-throb Norman Waller.

Royphillians at Burpham Village Hall. l - r: Roy Vinal, Norman Waller (class heartthrob), Ian Dopita and Phillip Goodhand-Tait (on piano).

KOSSACKS AND SHAKERS

l - r: Paul Demers, Joyce Todd, Wendy Baker (with monkey) and Phillip Goodhand-Tait.

The group was formed at George Abbot School and performed at Burpham Village Hall to an audience largely made up of pupils from the school and members of the Merrow Youth Club.

Youth clubs were an important part of teenage culture at this time. At Merrow, for example, there was table tennis and weightlifting for the boys. The girls had lectures on family matters, including visits from the Marriage Guidance Council. The only multi-sex activity was listening to 45 r.p.m. records on the Dansette record player.

After the Royphillians disbanded, a group developed under the extrovert leadership of singer Pete Tooley and his friend Paul Demers. Paul actually owned the drum kit, as his neighbours on the Bushy Hill estate would testify when he practised there, and his hero was Sandy Nelson. Pete had the Elvis look, but no musical prowess according to Phill. In fact, the group developed as a mime group, with Pete miming to tape recorded 45s and with two female backup singers, the Howard twins, also miming! This form of entertainment went down very well in Merrow where they were known, but was not quite so well received

43

GUILDFORD - THE ROCK'N'ROLL YEARS

in Horsham or Cranleigh!

Around 1961 the drummer Paul Demers was replaced by one Bert Curtis (later of The Age Beaters). Other changes in the group personnel included the recruitment of Dave Long to play bass and Gordon Rocket to replace Pete Tooley on vocals. The group now became known as Johnny Dark and The Midnighters. Phill started arranging bookings for them, the first being at the T.A. Centre in Woking. He eventually worked his way into becoming the group's vocalist. His parents allowed them to practice at home and the group now changed its name to Phill Tone and The Midnighters.

This group had its first gig at Eastleigh Town Hall. One of the groups who also played there at that time was Chevmoran and The Seekers. Phill was particularly impressed with their guitarist, Dick Middleton (see previous chapter). Apart from being an excellent guitarist, Dick had good equipment as his day job was at Sound City in Shaftesbury Avenue. Dick was already a professional musician and inspired Phill and his mates to strive for better things.

It was actually while Phill was still with The Royphillians that he was spotted by Kirk Riddle and Ivor Shackleton. In the summer of '61 Phill was performing at a talent contest at the Surrey County Show in a tent in Stoke Park. He had entered himself twice, once as a solo singer (performing a Jerry Lee Lewis song "Whole Lotta Shaking" and playing the piano) and once with the group.

At this talent contest Kirk and Ivor were performing with their then group The Dynamics. Kirk recalls the space behind the stage being somewhat congested, although he didn't actually complain that the band had to share this congested space with girls in their undies getting ready for a fashion show!

Kirk (real name Michael Frances) had been at the same junior school as Ivor in Moss Lane, Godalming. His dad, who was an aircraft engineer at Weybridge, was evidently also a competent amateur woodworker, first constructing an acoustic guitar for Kirk and then another one for Ivor. Kirk still has the guitar to this day and recalls it having a poor action, resulting in bleeding fingers. Kirk's dad, however, learnt by experience and the guitar for Ivor was a lot better!

Kirk and Ivor began to play in 1957, the peak year for skiffle, and later around 1959/60 formed their first proper band, The Dynamics, playing mainly instrumentals such as those by The Ventures. The Riddle family woodworking ability continues with Kirk manufacturing a solid bass guitar for Graham Cross to play and building cabinets for the small amps they were able to purchase through Exchange & Mart.

Kirk and Ivor were members of Farncombe Youth and at this stage played acoustic guitars and it was only subsequently when they decided to form a trio that it was decided mutually that Ivor, being the better musician, should play lead and Kirk, bass. Eventually, Phill, Ivor and Kirk decided to form a group, along with Phill's old friend the drummer, Paul Demers and so The Shakers were formed in October 1961. Thus the Farncombe/Merrow connection was established and Kirk and Ivor found themselves regularly travelling by bus over to Merrow for practice sessions. The journey involved carrying the guitars and amplifiers on the bus and changing at Guildford.

Ivor's first proper job was at a building site office in Haslemere, but the company went bust during the severe winter of 1962/63 and Ivor was laid off. He fancied the idea of being a ladies hairdresser and undertook a course on this subject in London. By this stage, The Shakers were well under way. Ivor recalls making phone calls about gigs in breaks between lectures, taking the train down from London to Guildford, being picked up and changing in the van on the way to the gig.

Trish, Ivor's girlfriend and wife to be, was a hairdresser. It may have been this that encouraged Ivor into the hairdressing profession, or possibly he thought it was an easier option than building work.

GUILDFORD - THE ROCK'N'ROLL YEARS

They first met when Trish attended her first gig, which happened to be

at the Godalming Youth Club's Valentine Dance, and the band playing happened to be The Shakers. Trish was already aware of Kirk and Ivor. She lived nearby and had frequently seen them loading and unloading the van, and here she was, aged 15, and receiving attention from Ivor, four years her senior.

Like many other teenage girls aged 14 or 15 at this time, there was a curfew. In her case, she had to be back in by 9 p.m. normally, although this was a special occasion.

During their early relationship there were inevitably difficulties with Ivor being away for fairly lengthy periods as a professional musician, but overall this was counteracted by the strong friendships formed with the other members of the band and their girlfriends.

The Shakers were certainly not a manufactured group. They did not start with top quality equipment. The very name "The Stormsville Shakers" was inspirational. They had the idea of acquiring leather waistcoats as their "uniform", if you can call it that, and slowly graduating from home-made equipment to cheaply bought second hand equipment and eventually the quality of gear that was necessary for the type of gigs they were commanding. Through this period, Kirk was working as a trainee engineer with Hambledon Rural District Council. His first bass guitar was a Fenton Weill, bought from Pete Tooley and the first proper bass amp an Ampeg.

Kirk and Ivor were a year older than Phill. Kirk had transport in the form of an Austin Princess. Paul had a day job and financed the 30-watt amplifier and two 12" Goodman speakers for this. The PA was augmented by a Watkins Copy Cat echo unit.

Phill says:

"The name Stormsville was taken from a Johnny and The Hurricanes album sleeve and Shakers, well we did shake up the places we played, but it was an in vogue expression of the time and the name of the dance style. Advertisements exhorted the youth of the day to nod and shake. It was pretty decadent! Youngsters, mainly girls, would nod and shake their bodies not too provocatively by today's standards, rooted to one position, in a circle with their handbags in the middle, while the boys hung around the perimeter of the dance hall, drinking beer or cider and eyeing up the talent. There was no need to interrupt good drinking time until the last dance, necessarily the moment to choose your preferred girl to walk home with."

Author's note: *I was aware of Kirk and Ivor, as they were fairly high profile pupils (although they would probably in modesty deny this) at Godalming Grammar School, where I also was a pupil but some years younger. The first time I saw The Shakers - and, in fact, this was probably the first proper rock group I had seen - was in December 1962 at Guildford Tech. They were certainly not loud by today's standards, but I do recall the Head of Science having some comments about the decibel levels!*

There is a story about Kirk and Ivor at Godalming Grammar School. They were both great cross-country runners. The association

GUILDFORD - THE ROCK'N'ROLL YEARS

of these two and cross-country running always puts me in mind of Eddie Cochran's "The Tortoise and The Hare", except that in this case they were both hares. On one famous occasion, they both came in joint first in the school cross-country run, after Kirk had nobly waited for his friend and rival to be sick!

Ivor and Kirk, school buddies from Godalming

On 5th May that year the band were travelling down to Portsmouth Guildhall to see Jerry Lee Lewis, and Johnny Kidd and The Pirates. Phill recalls them having a "top heavy" van, driven and owned by Paul Demers. The van turned over and went into the ditch. "We could have all been killed" said Phill. Fortunately, none of them were even injured, apart from Phill's girlfriend who had a cut head.

There is something classically simple about the guitar, bass and drums trio and no doubt the early Shakers would have been influenced by The Pirates, who were probably the best exponents of that format at the time. Kirk also cites Vince Taylor and The Playboys as a significant influence.

Just before Christmas 1962, two 15-year-old girls from Guildford High School organised an Oxfam Charity Dance at Holy Trinity Hall.

KOSSACKS AND SHAKERS

The Shakers played and gave their services for nothing. The concert was written up in the Surrey Advertiser. This provided fabulous publicity for the group, and led to a lot of bookings. It effectively launched them.

♪♫

In 1963 was held the heat of The Red Cross Rock - Trad Band Contest, when The Kossacks came out on top. Dave Brice, perhaps understandably, took exception to Surrey Advertiser reporter Mark Ackerman's words that:

"When the marks of the three judges were added together, The Kossacks were given a points victory, but if audience reaction had been the only factor taken into consideration, there is no doubt that The Shakers would have delivered a knock-out blow".

The report neatly summed up the kind of music each band played:

"Although The Kossacks and The Stormsville Shakers both came under the category of rock groups, their approach and style could not be much further apart. The Kossacks concentrate on a slick pop sound and score on the versatility side by having a female singer as well as the usual singing guitarist.

"If you called The Shakers slick they would be offended. Theirs is the wild, original rock sound that is gaining favour at the moment through such singers as Chuck Berry and Bo Diddly."

This competition was organised by the Surrey branch of the Red Cross as a rock and trad contest. This would now, and probably did then, seem an odd combination. Writing to the Surrey Advertiser at the time, L. Williams of Godalming said that there should have been separate sections for the trad bands and the rock groups. "Take the amplifiers away from the rock groups and they are finished. The rock groups are not musicians, they are electricians."

According to Dave Sherrington (later of The Stormsville Shakers), his was the only jazz band playing. In fact, it went under the name of Dave Sheridan's Jazz Band and the number they played was "Mood Indigo" by Duke Ellington. The fact that they were probably the best musicians on show (not Dave's words) but came last, obviously did nothing to change Dave's disdain for rock'n'roll at this time (see next chapter).

There was an advert in the Surrey Advertiser for entrants for the competition to be held with heats over four weeks between 15th April to 15th May and a final on 25th May. It would appear that there was also a semi-final stage and that by some odd quirk of organisation (or possibly deliberately) The Kossacks and Shakers met at all three stages of the competition. The results of their meetings would appear to be that The Kossacks were judged winners in the heat, as controversially reported above (although both groups appear to have gone through to the semi-final) and that The Shakers won both the semi-final and final. Also in the heat featuring these two bands was another Guildford band, The Crescents, featuring Colin Mills (lead guitarist), Brian Avery (rhythm guitarist), Ian Cooper (bass guitarist) and Laurie Way (drummer). This heat comprised five entries and the final of the competition four competitors, including two groups from the Purley area.

The Crescents

According to David Rose and Bernard Parke in "Guildford: Remember When" published by Breedon Press, 2007,

"There was a bit of argy-bargy when The Shakers and Kossacks met for the second time in the semi-final of a music contest. It was in 1963 and the venue was The Plaza Ballroom. The story in the following Wednesday's mid-week Surrey Advertiser began: "We would have liked to have shown you on this page a picture of two rock bands shaking hands with one another. But after the results were announced, Dave Brice, leader of The Kossacks, somehow didn't seem interested. Actually, his exact words were: "You won't get me posing for any photos with them" - meaning his rivals, The Shakers."

"The report added that there were some wild accusations going around that the judges were biased. However, the reporter, believed to have been Mark Ackerman, may have used his journalism skills to flam up the whole episode. Both bands went on to play the final, held at Shalford Park on Saturday, 25th May, 1963, but there was to be no luck in store for The Kossacks. When they went on stage to play their set, the generator supplying the electricity packed up".

In Dave's words:

"The generator broke down in the middle of the best song. Although it was eventually re-started the moment was lost. To this day I am convinced that someone deliberately sabotaged that generator and I would like to know who. Having said that, The Shakers probably deserved to win. They were a very good group, less middle of the road than us. They were the sound of the future."

For various reasons, in January 1964 Dave left The Kossacks. By this time he was engaged to be married. He also had a good "proper job", now with the civil engineers Connaught Contractors and worked in various locations around the country.

Dave owned a very good PA system, which he had had specially made by P.J. Equipment - a Vortexian, comprising two 40 watt amps with Goodman speakers, providing unheard power at the time. This equipment was so good that professional bands they were supporting often asked to use it. Dave now sold the PA to The Chris Allen Band and his Premier drum kit to Bert Curtis of Woodbridge Road, who was now starting out with the Age Beaters (see Chapter 7).

The Kossacks folded about nine months later, but Dave continued to play occasionally in a jazz band with his brother-in-law.

There is a happy ending to the so-called "argy bargy" of the Red Cross competition, in that Dave Brice and Phillip Goodhand-Tait shook hands when they met 45 years later at a dinner organised by Phill and Dave Sherrington.

David Brice (left) shaking hands with Phillip Goodhand-Tait Christmas 2008, Milford

Chapter 4
Shakers become Circus

During 1963 The Shakers played a total of 130 gigs, nearly all within a 10 mile radius of Guildford. In '64 more gigs were played, including as far a field as The Whiskey A-Go-Go Club in Newcastle. By '65 the gig list was up to around the 200 mark and in '66 over 250, including a residency at The Palladium Club, Paris.

For the early part of the existence of The Shakers, from '61 to '63, Phill was working during the day at a bank in London. By his own admission, he was often tired during the day, but managed to snatch some sleep in the toilets or during the extended lunch hour!

Part of the prize for winning the competition at Shalford Park was an audition for a recording contract at Decca. The audition took place on 21st February, 1964, with the recording test on 28th April of that year. Decca turned them down. This turned out to be no disgrace, however, as the person who turned them down was the same person who declined to offer The Beatles a contract.

1964 was the height of the beat groups, with such as The Searchers and The Swinging Blue Jeans coming to fame. It is therefore perhaps ironic that right at the beginning of 1964, The Shakers decided to move away from any image they might have had as a beat group. The big decision was made to add a saxophone to the line up and eventually two saxes. The Shakers had seen the sax player Steve Howard with another band and liked the way he moved - The Shakers had already added some steps to their performance.

On 17th January Steve Howard, tenor sax, joined The Shakers to create a five- piece unit. Very shortly afterwards, Paul Demers decided to leave the band. He had been one of the founder members, but as well as not particularly liking the new sound, he was getting married, still holding down a job in the Co-op Bakery Accounts Department, and decided that marriage was not compatible with the touring and other aspects of life in a rock group.

On 8th February Dick Forcey became the new drummer. Forcey was yet another art school product - this time Guildford Art School. The art schools certainly seemed to have produced more musicians than artists. With no disrespect to Paul Demers, it is Kirk's view that Dick was a step up as a technician and got the job after other candidates had been auditioned.

The Shakers had decided to base themselves on Cliff Bennet and The Rebel Rousers and to become part of the London R & B scene rather than a beat group as such. The leading practitioners on the London scene were Georgie Fame and The Blue Flames, The Zoot Money Big Roll Band and Chris Farlowe and The Thunderbirds, all well known names on that scene, but none perhaps receiving the same fame and recording recognition as some of the Liverpool beat groups.

On 11th July, 1964, The Shakers became a six-piece, with the

GUILDFORD - THE ROCK'N'ROLL YEARS

addition of Peter ("Greg") McGregor on tenor sax. Greg was recommended by Dick Forcey. Most of the R & B soul bands with two saxes, in fact had one tenor sax and one baritone sax. The Shakers decided on a slightly different sound with the two tenors. Also around this time, Phill recommenced his piano playing career with the acquisition of an electric piano.

SHAKERS BECOME CIRCUS

Asked whether or not he was the leader of the band, Phill says:

"When there were four of us it was easier to make group decisions, but when we became six, someone had to be the leader and, I guess if anybody, that was me. It was, however, mainly Ivor and Kirk's idea to add saxes".

Musically, therefore, The Shakers were applying their instincts and interests in expanding the band, but commercially this was not an immediate success. In fact, quite the contrary. The money had to be divided six ways and they were all a little bit worse off. On the other hand, the expanded line up opened new avenues for them with regard to the quality and quantity of gigs they were able to obtain.

Kirk, Ivor and Phill were all going steady at this stage and they were all thinking about leaving work to turn pro. Greg was the only one not working a 9-5 job and he said that the band needed better paid work, an aggressive agent and recording contract or he would need to re-consider his position with the band.

Tensions were therefore developing within the band in late 1964, particularly about the potential for going pro. Phill, as the ostensible leader of the band, had to take some difficult action for a 19-year-old. He had to deal with Ken Brewer of The Plaza and tell him that they were no longer prepared to work for £10 a night. Around this time they were approached by the Gunnell Agency, who ran The Flamingo Club. They wanted an exclusive contract on The Shakers, but couldn't guarantee the quality or quantity of work they needed. Phill reckoned that they needed to earn £120 per week to turn pro.

Turn pro, however, they did. It would appear that they would need to be working every night of the week to achieve their £120, particularly as a number of the gigs were in different parts of the country, involving additional travelling and accommodation costs. "Life was never more precarious" according to Phill.

Kirk says that he, as driver, got £18 a week and the others £15, the balance (if any) being put in the bank. They had run the wage system for some time, which had already enabled them to buy a new van. By this time there were, however, financial problems in that they were not always able to pay themselves even this minimum wage. Greg was falling out with them over the system and wanted the net profit from each gig to be fully split. This precarious situation continued into 1965, when economies had to be taken such as driving 300 miles home from Newcastle and arriving at 6 a.m. in the morning rather than paying out on hotel bills.

It is just as well that Kirk liked (and still likes) driving. He also later had the job of driving their new sax player, Jeff, to and from his home in north London for every gig. Despite the horrendous hours, the band never got into the use of amphetamines. They must have had some stamina.

Phill had met his steady, Joyce Todd, at the end of 1960. Between then and 1964, Kirk had met Bernice and Ivor had met Tricia.

"During 1964" says Phill "the heat was on all three of us to make a commitment. The girls wanted marriage and we guys wanted to be rock stars and you wouldn't be a rock star if it were known you were married. Female fans demanded to be in with a chance!".[1]

In September 1964 Peter "Greg" McGregor left The Shakers to be temporarily replaced by Jeff Cooke. On New Year's Eve that year they broadcast live on "New Year Revels" on the BBC Light programme. The following year, in February, David Sherrington and Tony Hurley replaced Jeff Cooke and Steve Howard on tenor saxes. Jeff and Steve had left to work on the boats, presumably for more financial security, Steve already having had experience of this type of work.

---

[1] Around '64/'65 Phill finally split with Joyce, but Kirk and Ivor went on to marry their steadies, Ivor and Tricia still being together to this day after well over 40 years. At the age of 21 Phill married Pearl and they had two kids together.

♪♫

SHAKERS BECOME CIRCUS

Dave Sherrington's history is that his mum and dad had been evacuated to Farncombe during the war and Dave was born soon afterwards in Godalming. At age 12 in 1955 Dave contracted T.B. and was confined to hospital for a long period. It was suggested that for him to take up a wind instrument would be good for his lungs. His mum bought him a cheap imitation plastic clarinet from Woolworths and he immediately fell in love with the instrument. He began to practice three or four hours a day under the tuition of one Ernest Doe.

There was a musical background in that his dad had been a piano player in pubs and for the silent films and had a great ear for music. His mum was also by all accounts quite a character.

The family were into all types of music, with Dave particularly influenced by dance band music and jazz. Dave went part time to Guildford School of Music, just off the Portsmouth Road, where he achieved Grade 8 classical music on the clarinet. He could therefore read music from an early age. From there he went part time to The Royal Academy of Music in London, with the intention of achieving the LRAM and becoming a classical clarinetist.

At the same time as all this was happening, however, he was playing in a dance band from the early age of 14. Says Dave:

"We all had to wear evening dress. My mum took me to Eddie Diamond, a Jewish retailer in Onslow Street, who fitted me up with a dinner suit. The line up of the band was piano, guitar, accordion, clarinet and drums. The leader did not play an instrument, but stood at the back handing out sheet music and announcing "Next dance, please!".

It was at one of this band's gigs in Leatherhead that Dave met a saxophonist who was with another band on the bill and who suggested that he have a go at the sax. Says Dave:

"It was one of those life changing moments. I took to it immediately. I even played the second half of the gig on the sax, never having played it before - as it was jazz and improvisation it was not so difficult!

"Within weeks I had bought my own alto sax and was completely sold on the sax. My mother was heartbroken. This was the end of my safe classical career.

A little later on, when I was living with my first wife at her parents' house, her dad was also concerned about the insecurity of the musical path I had chosen. One day he even said to me 'You've got a driving licence haven't you? I've found you a proper job. I've had to give out a few favours to get it for you. It's pushing the Council hand roller.' I looked in disbelief. I searched his face. He was deadly serious!"

Getting back to the more serious matter of playing the sax, this according to Dave is a natural double instrument for a clarinet player. Dave was a jazz fan and somewhat disdainful of pop music. When he first heard "Heartbreak Hotel" he thought it was crap. He liked Chris Barber, and Lonnie Donegan being part of the Chris Barber band was in Dave's estimation somewhat better than Elvis and the other rock'n'roll artists. The jazz which Dave played at this time was mainly mainstream and swing and the gigs were such as the art colleges.

Dave had a number of temporary jobs (not including pushing the Council roller), one of which was at Harveys (now the House of Fraser). He was aged 17 and had just passed his driving test. The first thing he was told to do was to collect the furniture van from Walnut Tree Close and bring it back to the store. This he did, but unfortunately he was not warned about the arch leading to the loading bay and the van got stuck under this. With much pushing and pulling and deflation of tyres it was freed.

By 1963 the Dave Sheridan Jazz Band was in full swing. For his stage name, Dave had reverted to his true family name. His ancestry was Irish and his great grandfather, who was illiterate and spoke in a broad Irish accent, was misunderstood by the Registrar following the birth of his son and went so far as to sign the birth certificate stating

SHAKERS BECOME CIRCUS

the name as Sherrington. It was only when Dave's father came to be enlisted in the army in the First World War, that he realised that his name was registered as Sherrington rather than Sheridan and Dave and his brother and sister were christened with the surname Sherrington.

Dave's first sighting of The Shakers was at the Red Cross Trad and Rock Contest at The Plaza. It was not until nearly two years later that he received a phone call from Kirk Riddle that they needed a new sax player. He is convinced that he was their last choice, being regarded as an old jazzer. He had known Kirk and Ivor when they were all in the same year at Moss Lane Primary School, but had lost contact when Kirk and Ivor went to the grammar school and Dave went to Meadrow Secondary Modern. Dave was obviously a highly intelligent chap and must have been a very marginal case for 11 plus failure, although as he said at that time he was very rebellious and probably would not have benefited from a grammar school education. Later in life, he became a mature student at Guildford Tech, Brighton University (where with The Shakers he had incidentally played one of the inaugural concerts) and Vancouver.

On joining The Shakers, Dave lost his disdain for rock music and loved some of the stuff which The Shakers were doing, including numbers by James Brown and Ray Charles. "I thought Phill had a terrific voice. I was knocked out by this and how professional the band were. They took their music very seriously." He also needed a permanent job. They did a few rehearsals at The Ricky Tick in Windsor and with Tony Hurley also joining on tenor sax, the latest Shakers' line up was underway.

♫♪

In April 1965 the American rock'n'roll legend, Larry Williams, visited England, to be backed by The Stormsville Shakers on tour. He had composed such rock'n'roll greats as "Dizzy Miss Lizzy", "Boney

61

Maroney", "Short Fat Fanny", "Slow Down" and "She Said Yeah". Larry played the piano and sang and brought with him his own guitarist, Johnny "Guitar" Watson.

Johnny "Guitar" Watson led the band, set the tempos, put in the solos and entertained everyone on and off stage with his humour. Phill was very much in the background, playing electric piano. Ivor also had to take a back seat in playing rhythm.

Phill felt that the agent who organised the tour was exploiting Larry and The Shakers. They were performing for a flat fee all over the country and the only way to make a little extra was to do a deal with a promoter to play an extra set after midnight. There was a problem when this once occurred in Manchester, when Larry wanted to do an extra set after midnight, but The Shakers had to be in Hastings the next day at The Witchdoctor Club. Therefore, the boys left without the illustrious duo, who were backed by a local band.

The Shakers travelled separately to Larry and Johnny to and from the gigs. According to Ivor the two stars spent ages in the dressing room getting ready, but "they were sharp dressers". They particularly liked Dick Forcey's drumming. It was handy that The Shakers already knew the numbers and did not have to "wing it". All in all, they did a professional job.

On the Monday, Larry and the boys were in the studio at Decca. They made an album, recorded in a day. The Shakers were paid the princely sum of £128.10s and received a credit on the album sleeve. The cover photo for the album was taken at The Plaza Ballroom, Guildford.

Larry Williams' backing band in America was Little Richard's backing band. There certainly appeared to be some similarities in sound between The Stormsville Shakers, as heard on this Decca record, and the old Little Richard songs, although possibly The Shakers did not swing quite so well on this studio album. Little Richard had of course done it back in the fifties. As Phill said by now "rock'n'roll had lost its shine".

Shortly after this recording, Larry agreed to make an album for Sue Records. The new album was duly made, with The Shakers still backing. It was intended to sell as a live album. In fact, there were 20 invited guests, led by cheerleader Screaming Lord Sutch and three songs were recorded at a time. The venue was The Marquee Recording Studio. This time The Shakers were paid about half the previous fee, £67.10s and did not receive any credit on the album sleeve. The result, however, was a barnstorming record, in Phill's opinion superior to the Decca recording.

♪♫

Phillip recalls why Mick Douglas had to stand in for Ivor Shackleton. The latter had been seriously injured in an incident at one of the group's gigs. Phill says

"It was at one of the ABC dances. During the break Ivor was with his mates, one of whom got picked on by a gang. Ivor doesn't back down. He stepped in, but had his jaw broken for his troubles. He subsequently had to have his jaw wired and eat Complan through a straw. With hindsight I was perhaps rather cruel in that I said that he could not come on the stage looking like that!

"Dougo was quite a character. He introduced us to Chris Andrews and this was as near as damn it that we got to having our life changing hit record. The song that Chris had for us was "Long Live Love". This was recorded at the Regent Sound Studios in London on 18th May, 1965. We did an arrangement and the demo and we played it at our gigs. It went down a storm. It was a blue beat song. We could play it at The Flamingo Club and the American black guys liked it. We could play it at the youth clubs and the teenyboppers would like it. It had an effect on people. It was a hit, there was no doubt about it.

"Chris Andrews was managed by Evie Taylor, who also managed

Sandie Shaw. Evie said that she could not give it to this unknown group, The Stormsville Shakers. Sandie Shaw was an established star and she got the song. The arrangement was identical, although played by session musicians. It was a number one hit."

Chris Andrews wrote and played lead guitar on a number of hit songs for Adam Faith. Dougo had played lead guitar on two tracks "We Are In Love" and "The First Time", recorded in 1963 and 1965 respectively and appearing on Adam's album "The Best of Adam Faith". Evie Taylor, as well as managing Chris Andrews, managed Adam Faith and according to Adam Faith's autobiography this was certainly not an easy relationship. [1]

Dougo had initially met Chris Andrews when they were playing together in the Pete Chester Combo (see chapter 1).

Dougo during his brief sojourn with The Shakers.

Phill says "After this disappointment (not getting the hit song) I knew then that we had to write our own material. Chris Andrews

[1] "Acts of Faith", Corgi Books, 1997.

really was an influence, showing me how it could be done." It was in fact while Ivor was in hospital that he was told that the band was going to go professional. He never went back to his hairdressing work.

According to the notes included with their latest CD (Phillip Goodhand-Tait and The Stormsville Shakers 1965 and 1966 and Ricky Tick 40 years on - Angel Air - 2005 and 2008. The sleeve notes were written by Nick Dalton in December 2007)

"The band's recorded output was limited to say the least. It was 1966 before they recorded under their own name, an E.P. of four Goodhand-Tait songs, on the French label Odeon/EMI. Achieving little, it did at least bring Phillip to the notice of Dick James, publisher of Northern Songs and Beatles fame, who signed him to a three-year songwriting deal. On May 6th, Parlophone released the first single by The Stormsville Shakers with Phillip Goodhand-Tait, "Gonna Put Some Hurt On You", previously released in America by Alvin Robinson and recorded at the legendary R. G. Jones Oak Records Studio in Morden, Surrey. The single made no. 40 in the Melody Maker charts in June 1966. Subsequent singles "No Problem" and "You Can't Take Love" couldn't even reproduce that success and marked the end of The Shakers recording career."

Phill says

"But even this small success ("Gonna Put Some Hurt On You") was not all it seemed. In fact, our management had made an arrangement to ensure that the record entered the charts. I am not privy to the details, but it was common practice at the time and involved the music publishing rights to the 'B' side of the disc and Radio Luxembourg, the influential pop radio station. Some money was paid to ensure that our debut single was a hit. This practice often did create genuine hits, if the management kept paying to keep the record in the lower reaches because, eventually, if the record had appeal, the public would hear it and buy it. In our case, however, the money only stretched for three payments and the record peaked at no. 40. Since I had not been the writer for either side of this single, I had no interest in the music publishing returns."

As a pure musician (as opposed to composer), Kirk never received any royalties for recordings. He received fees for the Larry Williams gigs and one little known fact is that he was even co-composer with Dave Sherrington on a 'B'-side instrumental entitled "J. C. Greaseburger", which became the introduction to a television programme in Venezuela!

♫♪

The huge disappointment felt by the band and those close to them over the "Long Live Love" episode was partly instrumental in the temporary break-up and Ivor's final disappearance from the band to take up a safe job in Guildford Council Architects Department. Around this period the personnel in The Shakers varied somewhat and, for a short period, also included two ex-members of The Bumblies - Goff on keyboards and Richard Hodby on drums.

The Shakers had, in fact, temporarily disbanded for about six weeks during the summer of '65. August is always a lean month for musicians. Dave and Kirk were working on a building site when Dave mentioned that his friend Chris Cassap could get them some work and that they should consider reforming. Ivor had already left and it was at this stage they enlisted Ian Jelfs and brought back Tony Hurley and Phill Tait. Ian was a near neighbour of Kirk's. He was a good musician, a good laugh and fitted in well with the band. Although for this very brief period Kirk had been enforced to give up work as a musician, he confesses that music was (and always has been) his life.

On 30th October, 1965, Ian Jelfs replaced Ivor Shackleton on lead guitar. Ivor was finding it increasingly difficult to reconcile his marital situation with life on the road. Kirk, on the other hand, although still going steady with Bernie (who he was eventually to marry), never in his words "felt any pressure to do or not to do anything!".

Author's note: *Ian was yet another pupil at Godalming Grammar School. He was two years younger than me, and a year older than Stuart Reffold (see chapter 9). He was an excellent sportsman and I first met him and his mate, Bob Wiles, through cricket. Ian was blond and good looking and becoming an excellent guitarist first with The Cutaways. He was only 16 years old when he joined The Shakers. He developed a jazzy style of play, citing his main influence as being Wes Montgomery*

Godalming Grammar Under-15s cricket team, 1962. Ian Jelfs second from left front row. Yours truly third from right back row.

Also around this time, Dick Forcey quit the band to go to Australia and was replaced by Alan Bunn from Farnborough. Chris Cassap was an ex-actor who had inherited some money and had pretentions to emulate The Beatles famous manager, Brian Epstein. Phill says

"Unfortunately, Chris had almost no managerial experience. That didn't stop us from allowing him to be our Manager, although there was no written agreement between us. At the time I wasn't aware that he was homosexual and I just accepted Chris's generosity".

Dave Sherrington's recollections of Chris Cassap are that he was an artistic type of person, a failed actor, but a great jazz fan - Dave had known Chris since before The Shakers. Chris ran a bar in Jeffries Passage and one of his employees was Sev Lenkevic, who later in the seventies played with the Guildford band Head Waiter and also Mungo Jerry. In the seventies Chris moved to Brighton and opened up a restaurant and bed and breakfast.

Cassap, however, did some good for The Shakers. He partnered Steven Komlosi in a new booking agency, Kacey Artistes Management, who in December 1965 booked The Shakers to play in Paris at La Locomotive Club. They were a great success.

In May 1966, Mel Collins (later of King Crimson) replaced Tony Hurley on sax. Again, this is a case of a band member leaving for a more reliable wage - in Tony's case, as a musician in the army.

THE STORMSVILLE SHAKERS
with
PHILLIP GOODHAND TAIT

l - r: Dave Sherrington, Ian Jelfs, Mel Collins, Phillip Goodhand-Tait, Kirk Riddle, Alan Bunn

SHAKERS BECOME CIRCUS

Of many of the incidents involving Ian and other members of the band, Dave Sherrington recalls:

"We were staying in an old hotel in La Chapelle, a run down area of Paris. Ian was so good looking, all the girls flocked round him. The old landlady of this hotel had to warn us that she was appalled by the number of girls going up to Ian's room. She asked me if I could have a word with Ian about it. She was worried that it would give her hotel a bad reputation. The fact that the whole area was a red light district seemed to be lost on her.

"We were a boozy lot. Ian couldn't handle the booze. To some extent we were responsible for that. There was one occasion when we were playing at a party at a huge golf club just outside Paris. Foolishly, the organisers had arranged for drinks to be available for the band - you just don't do that. Maybe a couple, but not bottles of champagne! We all got totally blotto! When we started to play, Ian was leaning against the wall because he could not stand up and he just

69

GUILDFORD - THE ROCK'N'ROLL YEARS

started slithering down the wall.

"We did an amazing series of gigs, including a residency at The Palladium in Paris. The agency really got their money's worth. We were actually sometimes doing three or four gigs a day. We had no money. We were starving. We had a good time by and large, but it was not glamorous. I was in a queue for some food once at a café. I

70

slipped a piece of chicken in my pocket, ate another piece of chicken and by the time I got to the checkout I only had a glass of water and a bread roll on my tray. The bloke behind the till said "Don't kid me, mate, I seen you put that chicken in your pocket - fuck it, good on you." What a lucky break that was, I could've ended up in jail."

The trips to Paris involved going in the van to Lydd airport, putting the van on a Bristol freighter aircraft on which they travelled to Le Touquet, driving from there to Paris, and then the same afternoon doing two gigs, followed by a further three in the evening, the last of which was recorded. Considering the day's work they had already undertaken, the recording was remarkably good.

Dave continues:

"We were very rarely a support group and certainly never in Guildford, but when playing with The Who in Paris, we were inevitably the support. I remember one occasion when Keith Moon did his obligatory kicking over of the drums and their roadie then went looking for another kit to replace it and found the one belonging to our drummer, Alan Bunn. Alan wasn't too keen on his kit receiving the treatment and the roadie had to do his best to reassemble Moon's kit or what was left of it.

"It was after one tour of Italy and followed by a short tour of Scotland that I realised my system would not keep up with the lifestyle we were leading - lack of sleep and plenty of booze (but no drugs - we could not afford it). I left The Shakers and for a few months never wanted to play again. In the event, I did of course play again on a semi-pro basis with various bands, including Jacky Lynton and The Baggy White Suit Band in the seventies."

Shortly before Dave left, there was a fall-out between Dave and Phill, although both agreed to carry on pro tem, as long as Kirk agreed to run the band.

♫♪

By the late 1960s The Shakers decided to go for a different image. This was the era of the much longer hair and flowery shirts. Many songs around this period were written under the influence of LSD, but not by Phill. Alcohol was more his scene than drugs. Phillip could not write psychadelic lyrics -"It was all tosh", but he could certainly write love songs.

With Dave having left, the band continued with Mel as the sole sax player. Mel introduced the strobe light and in Kirk's words "we had a kind of freak out" at The Marquee.

The band changed its name to Circus on 20th September 1967. Phill says:

"What was becoming apparent was that the band's sax heavy sound was out of kilter with what was happening in Britain at the turn of 1967, the year of Sergeant Pepper. When we changed our name to Circus in the summer of 1967 we were getting desperate. We embraced psychadelia, the tenor players changed to flutes, and we put on kaftans and threw flowers around. By the end of '67 we completely sold out, even though we were writing our own material. It sounded drug influenced, but none of us took drugs. It was silly.

"Circus made two singles, one of which was my path to future success. "Gone Are The Songs Of Yesterday" was covered by Love Affair for the 'B' side of "Everlasting Love". I knew nothing about it until it was out. Then the money poured in to me as the songwriter, driving a wedge between me and the rest of the band. That's how we broke up really."

Flower power.

The Shakers (now Circus) Fan Club Secretary was Doreen Pettifer, based at 86 Furze Lane, Godalming. In the newsletter of July 1967, she wrote of their return from their month-long visit to Italy, where they were not keen on the food and all had lost weight. Also Ian's Hendrix hairstyle had vanished and both Mel and Phill had shorter hair. The new name Circus was chosen by their manager, Chris Cassap, during their stay in Rome. The article announced the issue of their first record under the new name - "Gone Are The Songs Of Yesterday" on Friday, 8th September.

Other recordings included "What More Do You Want?" and "A Day Without Love" (the lyrics were about Phill and Joyce, his first girlfriend). "Gone Are The Songs Of Yesterday" by Phillip Goodhand-Tait was produced by Mike D'Abo and the 'B' side "Sink Or Swim" was composed by Mike. Mike also produced the subsequent record "Do You Dream".

According to Alan Bunn:

"The name Circus originally suggested was The Travelling Circus, but we wanted something snappy, so decided to do a little amputation on the name suggested by Mike D'Abo". The initial line up of Circus was Alan Bunn (drums), Mel Collins (sax and flute), Kirk Riddle (bass), Ian Jelfs (guitar) and Phill (vocalist)."

Phill continues:

"Ironically, Love Affair were doing what The Stormsville Shakers had been trying to do. They were starting to succeed basically doing orchestral versions of R & B. But they had two things going for them which we didn't. Firstly, they had an orchestra and the band didn't play, it was all session musicians. Secondly, they had sex appeal, particularly in Steve Ellis, who could sing too! We were a desperate bunch of lads who thought we were above that sort of thing.

"What Love Affair did do, though, was steer me into a career as a songwriter. Having had a 'B' side, I was determined to write an 'A' side, and this I did first with the Love Affair's top ten hit "A Day

Without Love" and then with "Bringing On Back The Good Times."

The 'A' side of the fourth Love Affair single was "One Road", written by Phillip Goodhand-Tait. This reached no. 15 in the charts and was considered to be a failure in comparison to the four previous top ten hits. The fifth single was written by Phill jointly with John Cokell and was "Bringing On Back The Good Times". Phill wrote the body of the lyrics "almost tongue in cheek" as he says, every other line being a cliché. Nevertheless, the record reached no. 5 in the charts. Phill's first solo record was one that he had written for Love Affair "Love Has Got Hold Of Me".

It was 1st January, 1969, that Phill left the Circus to start his solo career, which was launched at The Café Royal in London. The Circus without Phill appeared regularly at The Marquee in Wardour Street and released an LP on Transatlantic Records (TRA207).

There followed solo success for Phillip in the 1970s while his songs were recorded by the likes of Roger Daltrey and Gene Pitney. Phillip gradually moved into video and T.V., producing live shows involving everyone from Cockney Rebel to the Fabulous Thunderbirds. As a solo artist, Phill once returned to Guildford to the Civic Hall, but his career now took him all over the world, including the U.S.A., almost entirely as a support act.

Phill admits that he himself had a low key stage presence. In his early days he had the advantage of the enthusiasm of youth. Later his introverted character showed through. He started off with the same opportunity as Elton John, both having recording contracts with Dick James in 1971. It was economic for Dick James to sign singer/songwriters and Elton knew how to sell himself.

Author's note: *I was at college in London between 1967 and '71. Initially, I was living near The Elephant & Castle and lodging with one of the roadies for Manfred Mann. He took me along for their rehearsals and I briefly met Mike D'Abo. He told me how he had to disguise his posh accent - it didn't do to have a posh accent in this business. It was also around this time that I was a regular attendee at The Marquee Club and saw Circus there, including Phillip Goodhand-Tait. I distinctly recall Phill swinging the microphone stand and nearly decapitating a member of the audience! A little later I saw Phill as a solo artist at Imperial College, London. Much later, in the 1990s, in Brighton I met Steve Ellis with The New Love Affair (none of the originals apart from Steve) and had the opportunity of talking to him about his early days, including the Goodhand-Tait songs.*

After Phill left, Circus auditioned for a new vocalist, one of whom turned up in cycling vest and shorts and whom they politely declined. Unable to find a satisfactory replacement for Phill, the band continued mainly with instrumentals, although Ian also took up the vocals, including on the above-mentioned album. Towards the end, Chris Burrows replaced Alan Bunn on drums.

Even at such prestigious gigs as The Marquee, money was poor. Bands were willing to play for paltry sums at such prestigious venues in the hope of getting better known. It was Dave Robertson, the new manager of Circus, who got them the Transatlantic album deal and also T.V. shows in Amsterdam and Brussels.

One of the bands with whom Circus regularly appeared at The Marquee was King Crimson. According to Kirk they were "a very slick outfit". In Easter 1970 Mel was recruited to King Crimson and that was the end of Circus.

In the years since then, Mel has moved to Cologne where he is still in the music business, Ian moved to Paris and Kirk carried on over the years in the music business, including with Jackie Lynton, ran a number of pubs, passed through a number of relationships, and despite a serious car accident is still very much alive and kicking and playing with Stuart Reffold in Straubenzee. After the break up of Circus, Kirk by his own admission became depressed and started drinking, although he did hold down a job for a short while with Andertons music shop before going out on the road again to France and Germany with Dougo's Rooty Tooty Band, including a spell which in some ways he regards as the best time of his life, with no responsibilities, playing in a bar and sleeping on a beach. It was during this period in the early seventies that his marriage to Bernie broke up. Tina, Bob Potter's daughter, was for some years Kirk's live-in girlfriend.

The best time in the sixties for both Kirk and Ivor was in the early days when they were packing the youth clubs in Guildford and according to Kirk "living on air". Later on became a struggle, particularly financially, although some money was made promoting their own gigs at The Stoke Hotel and Civic Hall and fun was had abroad on their various trips to the likes of France, Switzerland and Germany.

The sixties in Guildford coincided almost exactly with the life of The Shakers/Circus, as did the sixties nationally (and perhaps internationally) with the life of The Beatles. There the comparison ends, but the longevity alone of The Shakers/Circus compared with

GUILDFORD - THE ROCK'N'ROLL YEARS

other Guildford bands does to some extent justify the space given to them in this book.

For further information, see Phillip Goodhand-Tait's website www.pg-t.com.

Chapter 5
The Venues

The various venues in the Guildford area have, of course, been referred to elsewhere in the book, but the more significant of them are each given some separate space in this chapter, together with references to the main artists who appeared at them and the recollections of those who attended. Other venues not given specific space in this chapter include The Pig 'n' Tater in Cline Road; Merrow Village Hall; The Ministry of Agriculture, Fisheries and Food in Epsom Road; The Congregational Hall, North Street; Onslow Village Hall; The Royal Hotel, Stoughton; and Foxburrows Hall.

Although not strictly music venues, Guildfordian Tony Backhurst recalls an extensive café scene in Guildford - places to go on a Sunday afternoon for a frothy coffee - including The Bamboo, Joe Lyons, Henekeys and the Cardboard Café in Woodbridge Road where his mate Bergie used to hang out. In the evenings, after the pub, one of the two Indian restaurants in Guildford made a useful to finish to the evening - hopefully paying the bill afterwards rather than escaping out of the window or by whatever means were possible. Boxers, of course, was the hangout place for many of us, just as the local pub would be these days. Peter Arthur (see chapter 1) for one remembers going to Boxers for his lunch hour, because in his words "that's where all the au pair girls went!".

The University of Surrey opened in 1968. Led Zeppelin's first gig was here. A number of free festivals were held here at The Stag Hill Campus in the 1970s.

One of the girls from this era, who was a true aficionado of the Surrey and London rock scene, kindly made her diaries available for the purposes of this book.

She was fortunate in that her uncle worked at The Odeon Cinema in Guildford and she was able to obtain free tickets for concerts there, including The Beatles, as well as numerous signed publicity photographs. She was a pupil at Pewley and George Abbot schools.

The quality of acts performing at relatively small gigs in Guildford at that time is illustrated by entries in the diaries - Chris Farlowe at The Sandfield Terrace T.A. Hall in March 1964, The Rolling Stones and Chris Farlowe at The Plaza in the same month (admission 10s.).

When not attending evening gigs, the girls would meet at The Spiders Web coffee bar in Chertsey Street (later to become The Bamboo), lunch at Boxers or for further evening entertainment attend the Worplesden R & B Club. This club featured Cyril Davies, Long John Baldry and Rod Stewart. Chris O'Donovan writes on the internet:

"As schoolboys making our way into Worplesden Village Hall, The Wooden Bridge and The Plaza to see Cyril Davies (always looked as old as a bush to me), the other brilliant bands and the imported American blues greats …….. we must have looked odd. What wouldn't I give to be able to have a second look … the odd details (I do remember) do seem to be bizarre in retrospect. We were incredibly young and even getting to Worplesden was no easy task. I remember three of us riding out there on one Lambretta. We regarded Cyril Davies and co. as the definitive R & B band. I still find it hard to reconcile my memories of Rod Stewart and Long John Baldry from those days with what they metamorphosed into as pop stars. "

The Bamboo Coffee Bar was at 62 Chertsey Street in the early 1960s. Christine Johnson (nee Stratford) used to frequent The Bamboo.

"Teenagers from all over Guildford, including myself, flocked to The Bamboo Coffee Bar to listen to the juke box and play the pinball tables.

THE VENUES

"Unfortunately, it had a bad reputation. People either chose a different route into town, or at least passed by on the other side of the road.

"Looking back over the decades, especially by todays standards, this was unjustified.

"No alcohol was sold on the premises; anyone entering drunk was thrown out, even barred. Drug taking was unheard of. The place was closed by 9.30 p.m. weekdays and 10.30 p.m. at weekends. I can recall no trouble. The police, to my knowledge, were never involved.

"Entering the building, you were faced with a flight of uncarpeted, rickety stairs. At the top was a mirror where we girls back-combed and lacquered our hair into bushy-like hairstyles, applied lashings of mascara, white eyeshadow and pale pink lipstick.

"We drank frothy coffee, bottles of Coca-Cola and glasses of fresh orange from a container where a plastic orange bobbed. It was also trendy to drink ice-cold milk.

"Pin tables stood along the wall at one end of the building. We were expert at handling these machines, knowing just how to tilt the table to allow the ball to fall into the "free go" holes, without causing the table to 'void'.

"Loud music throbbed from the juke box situated at the other end of the room.

"Popular songs blared out onto the street. Roy Orbison's 'Running Scared', Elvis Presley's 'Return To Sender' and Del Shannon's 'Runaway', fuelling the adrenalin and setting the blood pulsing. We jived and twisted on the concrete floor, wearing holes into the soles of our stiletto-heeled shoes." (From the archives edited by David Rose, Surrey Advertiser, 18th October, 2002.)

Guildford musician Dave Reading remembers the sixties as a time of relative innocence. Rock'n'roll was simple and exciting and in its infancy and by todays standards under-produced. Sex education was virtually non-existent. There were no mobile phones, no personal computers or the internet.

One meeting place that Dave recalls is The Bar None in North Street, which in fact was a religious drop-in centre. Also The Vintners, which was a pub on the south side of North Street, at the junction with Swan Lane. One of its claims to fame in the late 1960s was that the blind American blues singer/guitarist, Doc Watson, played there.

The Guildford Odeon

The Guildford Odeon.

The book "American Rock'n'Roll - The U.K. Tours 1956-72" by Ian Wallis (publisher Music Mentor Books) lists the various artists on the package tours (which included the Guildford Odeon). Amongst the

THE VENUES

luminaries appearing there were Gene Vincent[1] and Duane Eddy (1960), The Everly Brothers, Billy Fury, Bo Diddley and Little Richard in 1963 and, of course, most famously The Beatles in the same year[2]. It is even said that The Beatles had a drink in The Rats Castle in Sydenham Road before the show.

Sara Redpath, later a receptionist at The Surrey Advertiser, remembers the event well. She said she was 13 at the time and went to the concert with her mother and her best friend. "I spent the week prior to the concert practising my screaming", she said.

She remembers the concert as being brilliant.

"We stood outside for ages afterwards banging on the toilet windows, hoping The Beatles would hear us and come out to sign autographs. Sadly, they didn't.

"The queue was long. It went right round the side of the building and up to Sydenham Road. "

Jackie Everett from Wood Street village, says:

"I think the management were quite taken aback with all the unruly behaviour. The Beatles concert seemed to set a precedent. After that it was the norm for people to scream and shout. Security then became much tighter."[3]

Around this time, 1962/63, the music was generally drowned out by the screaming. This type of female near hysteria went back to the fifties with Johnny Ray and Elvis Presley - look on YouTube for a

---

[1] Eddie Cochran would have appeared on this gig, had he not died a few months earlier.

[2] My brother John and I passed up the opportunity of seeing the Beatles, but certainly remember seeing The Rolling Stones well down on the bill at one of these concerts.

[3] From the archives, David Rose, Surrey Advertiser, 18th October, 2002.

1956 clip of Elvis singing "Heartbreak Hotel". It was in the late sixties and early seventies that the amplification was stepped up a gear and would certainly have counteracted any screaming!

Brian Hyland played at The Odeon in February 1963. The Surrey Advertiser reported "police with dogs", due to the behaviour of the fans and Brian Hyland barricaded in his dressing room. Betty Thornton of Barnes and Avis music shop (see next chapter), in fact, was in the dressing room! The reason appears to have been quite innocent in that her husband Mark had been interviewing Brian and earlier that day Brian had made a personal appearance at Barnes & Avis.

Ricky Tick/Plaza Ballroom

The Plaza is thought to date from around 1910. In the early days of cinema in Guildford this was known as The Picture Palace. The

THE VENUES

building has remained an entertainment venue to this day, including as a dance hall, bingo hall and now night club.

There were originally four cinemas in Guildford, the Playhouse in the High Street, the Odeon at the top of the High Street, the Cinema in Woodbridge Road and the Plaza in Onslow Street. The Plaza was known as The Bug Hutch at that stage. Dave Brice's mate was a junior projectionist at the latter and recalls it being the type of cinema attended by men in raincoats and showing a certain type of French film. However, it changed to a ballroom around 1957/58 and Dave's cousin became the Manager. Dave Brice's group, The Rhythm Five, were said to be the first to play there, supporting the Chris Allen Band, whose singer was Bobby Lambert. It was common at that time, for the main act to be a big band of the old fashioned type and the support to be a small group such as Dave's. Pretty soon the venue was to be run as the Ricky Tick Club.

Eveline Leonard (2005) reports on the Stormsville Shakers' web site:

"During the 1960s, the Ricky Tick Clubs were venues in the English home counties, in Windsor, Guildford, Croydon and Reading, that attracted teenagers to hear blues, rock'n'roll, jazz or rhythm and blues music, often all night and always at least five days a week. American stars brought over by U.K. agents to play nationwide tours would find themselves sub-booked to appear several sessions per night at different venues near London. The Ricky Tick Clubs, along with Eel Pie Island, London's Flamingo or Marquee Clubs were significant venues in this multi-gig moneymaking circuit.

"What distinguished a Ricky Tick Club from any other was firstly the presentation style. It was simplistic, ads rolled out by silk screen on black posters with crude white lettering and always using a very eye-catching logo - a huge Afro head shouting the blues, stencilled in white. A large mansion, in Windsor, not far from the castle and the Thames, became Philip Hayward and John Mansfield's Ricky Tick

GUILDFORD - THE ROCK'N'ROLL YEARS

Club headquarters and main venue. Windows were covered, walls painted matt black and the task of painting the Afro blues shouters in white on either side of the stage was undertaken by Hog Snort Rupert, a would-be designer, in return for living quarters in the boiler room and the occasional gig for his band.

"The Hog Snort Rupert Band were doing songs by James Brown, Bobby Bland and Larry Williams. They had sax players. His real name was Bob McGrath and he was a student at Farnham Art College, where poster arts with a pop influence were emerging.

"By 1964/66, a pattern of entertainment had been set up. U.K. Musicians' Union rules required that U.K. artists touring America had to be exchanged for U.S.A. artists performing in Britain. American blues exponents began to replace jazz musicians as U.K. youth sought out the original sounds from the American south. English groups such as The Yardbirds, Alexis Korner or The Rolling Stones, and particularly their guitarists, imitated the music of Robert Johnson, Muddy Waters and John Lee Hooker.

"What every visiting American name needed was a British back-up band. The Musicians' Union rules meant that it was too expensive or cumbersome to exchange back-up musicians in all but a few cases. Here was an opportunity for British bands to get close to their influences and learn from them first hand. Thus, John Mayall and his Blues Breakers accompanied John Lee Hooker, encouraging legendary British guitarist, Eric Clapton."

Peter Clayton in his article on Chris Barber describes bringing over American artists, including Big Bill Broonzy, Rosetta Tharpe, Sonny Terry and Brownie McGhee, Muddy Waters and Otis Spann, Jimmy Cotton and Louis Jordan.

"That the visitors have nearly all been singers, and that the one who wasn't a singer didn't come to Britain, is due to the baffling intricacies of the Anglo-American exchange system. You can bring in a vocalist; if you want an instrumentalist you got to send one to America in exchange. As you may have heard (but as the Musicians Union presumably has not), America is pretty well off for jazz soloists already, and we don't really have anybody they want. So in spite of doubts even within the band, Chris settled for vocalists, usually those who accompany themselves as well."

As noted in the previous chapter, Larry Williams' visit to the U.K. was the opportunity for The Stormsville Shakers to provide the backing.

Ricky Tick Club Poster Logo
designed by Hogsnort
Rupert

Jim Cook, later of Whisker Davis, recalls receiving an album by Blues Incorporated around 1961. Says Jim:

"This was a very influential British R & B band, probably the first of its kind. It struck an immediate chord with me, and of course with many more who went on to make the British R & B boom, including The Rolling Stones. How curious that R & B and blues music was to be so relevant and engaging to affluent suburban white kids, with no common experience with black, mainly middle-aged, oppressed musicians from segregated America."

The Ricky Tick Club at The Plaza, Onslow Street, did not sell alcohol and according to Jim, who was a regular attendee, he never saw any drugs. "It seemed very civilized with orderly queues each side of the doors and had a staffed cloakroom inside."

Amongst the most famous artists to appear there were Gene Vincent, The Rolling Stones, The Who, The Yardbirds with Eric Clapton, Trident with Jeff Beck, Alan Price, The Paramounts (soon to become Procol Harem) with Gary Brooker, The Steam Packet with Long John Baldry and Rod Stewart, and The Animals. Jim recalls one particular gig:

"Chicago city blues came to Guildford in the impressive shape of Howlin' Wolf, who strode up and down the tiny stage like a caged animal. Having seen The Wolf and his famous guitarist, Hubert Sumlin, as part of a blues review at Croydon the night before, I was surprised to see Hubert in the gents at The Ricky Tick at Guildford. I told him how much I had enjoyed the previous night, at which he was very pleased and insisted on shaking my hand. Unfortunately, he continued to urinate at the same time.

"Walking from Guildford station to The Ricky Tick, a dormobile van drew up alongside and asked for directions to the club. I was astounded to see that it was Bo Diddly asking me and I could see Jerome and The Duchess sitting in the van behind him.

"Queuing outside The Ricky Tick to see Sonny Boy Williamson, the crowd was delighted when Sonny Boy came busking along the street, dressed in his trademark grey and black chequer board suit and bowler hat."

Jim continues:

"On 28th August, 1963, The Ricky Tick Guildford was being held at Worplesden Memorial Hall and The Rolling Stones had been booked. There were, however, no Stones and no amplification either to plug the record player into. Philip Hayward was at The Ricky Tick, Windsor. Brenda Elsdon and David Woodrow, plus two bouncers, were at Worplesden trying to control the pandemonium.

"David, a school teacher by profession, took to the stage, and while assuring the audience that the Stones would be arriving soon, he told them stories, organised sing-songs and games. He then got people up on stage to do their party tricks. Brenda did her best to pacify the fans as well. There was no bar, but the caretaker and his wife made lots of cups of tea and orange squash for the fans.

"Complete refunds were made and finally people left in an orderly manner. What had happened was that earlier that day the Stones had recorded an appearance for the T.V. show, Ready Steady Go. The contract to appear at Worplesden had been signed long before the T.V. appearance came about. One of the bouncers had telephoned the B.B.C. only to receive confirmation that the Stones had finished making their recording and had left on time. But they just didn't bother to turn up at Worplesden. An apology was later made by Brian Jones and a spurious story about their van breaking down was given. It was later learnt that the Stones had instead decided to go to a trendy London night club to celebrate their T.V. appearance."

The T.A. Centre
The Guildford & Godalming Times of 13th September, 1963, reported on a talent contest at the T.A. Centre, Leepale Lane. The dance opened with Ricky Clayton and The Rhythmics, followed by The Stormsville Shakers, who accompanied all the entrants in the competition. Entrants included Terry Ward of The Bumblies, who was the winner. Second was Mick Maslin of The Night Hawks and third place went to two boys, Chris Coppinger and Rod Faulkner. The two girl entrants included Caroline Harms of The Kossacks and also Linda Smith of Guildford. The prizes were presented by Steve Perry, Guildford's own pop singer, who had recently joined The Bachelors. Steve Perry's real name was Doug Downs and he was from Bellfields Estate. He had several singles released from 1960. Steve had recently been given a leading part in the West End musical, Pocahontas, and had left the rehearsals in London to attend the competition. The

competition was judged by the volume of applause in the audience and this in turn was judged by Betty Thornton and her fiancé, Mark Ackermann.

The Jubilee Club
The Jubilee Club was in Onslow Street, on the opposite side of the road to the Plaza. There was a group of shops here including P.J. Equipment Hi-Fi shop. The club was owned by the Friary Brewery and was in fact their social club. Dave Brice's group, The Crescendos, rehearsed there. In fact, Dave recalls that his dad was a mate of the steward, who let them rehearse for nothing, provided that they played the occasional free gig.

The Wooden Bridge
This pub at the bottom of Woodbridge Hill was a regular venue for up-and-coming R & B artists, supported by local bands. The Rolling Stones played ten gigs in Guildford during 1963, including The Wooden Bridge pub, The Ricky Tick Club, The Civic Hall and The Odeon.

The Wooden Bridge was a good place to attend on a Sunday evening to see the bands and have a drink with friends and other band members.

Jim Cook recalls seeing The Jeff Beck Group there, featuring Ron Wood and Rod Stewart - "A very good show, hot and sweaty. Also saw Ten Years After featuring Alvin Lee, the speed guitar hero, who went on to wow the Woodstock Festival."

The Ricky Tick Organisation hired The Wooden Bridge and The Civic Hall for some of their gigs, together with The Worplesden Memorial Hall. The Ricky Tick web site says that

"9th March, 1963, was their opening night at The Wooden Bridge where The Rolling Stones had established a fantastic and fanatical support. Philip Hayward, co-promoter with John Mansfield, arrived at

THE VENUES

the pub about 7 p.m. to find the car park crammed full of Stones fans.

"Philip had recruited three new bouncers to work at Guildford. He quickly instructed them to open the back doors and for one of them to assist the Stones to unload their equipment. Then the bouncers had to secure all the doors and windows, so that the fans could not get in without paying. This would be highly illegal today and rightly so.

"Within a very short time the ballroom was packed. Once the Stones started playing, the response was predictable. The fans were foot stomping, hand waving and girls were perched on other people's shoulders."

"There were hundreds of fans locked outside. Suddenly, fire doors were ripped open and all these people started to pour in. The newly recruited bouncers had a struggle to maintain order, which they did with good humour and without resorting to violence.

"At the end of the evening, as Philip was paying the bouncers, he expected them to say they were not interested in further work at The Wooden Bridge. They looked like they had just survived a tornado. Their clothes were torn, but they were happy - and were looking forward to the following Friday!"

Pete Anderton, Tony Boast and Geoff Andrews at The Wooden Bridge, 1966.

GUILDFORD - THE ROCK'N'ROLL YEARS

<u>The Civic Hall</u>
The Guildford Civic Hall opened in 1962 among much pomp and ceremony on a night that the Surrey Advertiser described as "comparable to an event in London's West End".

Dignitaries from across the county were invited to the official opening and on 11th October enthusiastic audiences enjoyed the first public concert, a classical evening featuring renowned pianist, Garry Graffman[1].

It was the intention of the Borough Council to host what in their view were civilised concerts at The Civic Hall, classical, dance bands, etc. However, they could not hold back time, nor could they afford to. Rock concerts and dances were to become the norm. The artists were mainly local bands or from the London area, but also included more famous performers such as Ben E. King and Gene Vincent. Screaming Lord Sutch (later of parliamentary candidate fame) and The Savages performed[2].

In November 1963 The Stormsville Shakers were top of the bill for the fabulous sum of £5. The poster also indicates four groups to be playing that night, Phill and The Stormsville Shakers, The Original Dominoes, The Condors and The Age Beaters. The poster shows forthcoming events with The Age Beaters being the regular support group. Admission was 4/- for three hours of non-stop rock and twist from 8-11 pm. A bar and a buffet was advertised.

In the early sixties, The Civic Hall was host to Britain's first rhythm and blues concert, a seated show featuring The Graham Bond Organisation, The Yardbirds, Georgie Fame and The Blue Flames and

---

[1] From the archives, David Rose, Surrey Advertiser, 10th January, 2004.

[2] Sutch appeared with a toilet seat round his neck and a young man jumping onto the stage protesting that the show was utter rubbish and should not have been allowed.

THE VENUES

The Rolling Stones. Says Jim Cook: "A member of the audience went up on the stage and gave Mick Jagger half-a-crown for a haircut. Mick laughed and tossed it behind him. Keith Richards picked it up, bit it and put it in his pocket. There were no bouncers. A top show."

By the mid-sixties, The Civic Hall continued to attract top names, including Elton John, Eric Clapton, Marc Bolan and T-Rex, Gary Moore, The Move, P. P. Arnold, Fleetwood Mac, and decades later such as Fairport Convention and Mark Knopfler. It is a little known fact that the rock group, Free, wrote their all time classic hit "All Right Now" in a dressing room backstage at The Civic Hall.

6 July 1967

A charity event took place on 14th December, 1967 at Guildford Civic Hall. Topping the bill were Peter Green's Fleetwood Mac. Also on the bill was Duster Bennet (from Kingston). At that charity concert was the John Mayall Fan Club Secretary, Doreen Pettifer, who reviewed the acts appearing that night in a subsequent newsletter:

"The Blues Concert at Guildford's Civic Hall on December 14th

GUILDFORD - THE ROCK'N'ROLL YEARS

featured an artiste who is going to be very, very big. His name is Tony Bennet, a kind of one man band. He plays guitar and harp, bass drum and high-hat cymbal with his feet and he also sings - at the same time. He is a brilliant musician who must have a very bright future.

"Fleetwood Mac and The Ainsley Dunbar Retaliation were knocked out by him, and thanks to Peter's ravings to Mike Vernon, Tony is likely to be recorded by him in the near future. Watch out for him because he is one of the biggest "finds" in years."

Probably the most successful night that The Civic Hall knew was when Graham Andrews brought The Swinging Blue Jeans to Guildford, when their record "Hippy Hippy Shake" was riding high in the charts. At least 400 people were turned away and youngsters came from as far as London to see the group.

At the end of the eighties, one of the most popular bands on the local circuit was Sammy Rat's Big Big Blues Band. Between 1987 and 1990 they put in seven appearances at The Civic Hall. The lead singer was none other than the Surrey Advertiser archives editor, David Rose.

Gary Brooker, now living in the Guildford area, was born in Hackney in May 1945. He formed The Paramounts in the early sixties and Procol Harum in 1967. He was awarded the MBE on 14th June, 2003, and performed at the "last fling" at Guildford Civic Hall on 4th January, 2004, before it closed down. A few months prior to this in June 2003, another one of the "closing down" concerts featured reunions of Guildford groups, including Mick Douglas' Razzle Dazzle, The Phantom Four, The Switch and The Stormsville Shakers[1].

---

[1] It was my privilege to be a part of this show. What a strange but great feeling to be up there with my old mates from The Switch, after no less than 36 years, performing before 700 people, all of whom - believe it or not - had paid good money to attend and, if I say so myself, I think we all put on a decent show!

THE VENUES

Congregational Youth Club

Of the many youth clubs in the Guildford area, perhaps the Bellfields Congregational or "Congo" as it was known deserves special mention. Bellfields is of course the large Council estate in the northern part of Guildford, between the railway line and A320 Woking Road. It was developed just after the Second World War. The houses were typically well built for the period, relatively spacious and with good sized gardens. Amenities on the estate included large open spaces and two youth clubs, one the St. Peter's Church of England Club and the other The Congregational Church Club. Many important local groups appeared there, including The Stormsville Shakers and Ricky and The

GUILDFORD - THE ROCK'N'ROLL YEARS

Secrets. The Surrey Advertiser of the time reports as follows:

"One of the most successful and hardworking youth clubs in the Guildford area is Stoke Hill Congregational Club. It owes its success wholly to one person - a young man who attended the club for some years and saw that it was rapidly running downhill with membership dropping as low as 25 - 30 about 18 months ago. He took it upon himself to rebuild the club, starting from the beginning.

"He is John Handby, the 19-year-old leader of the club, who has rallied it to the extent that membership now numbers over 100, with a waiting list of about 70 - and it recently won the drama award during the Youth Festival with a play which John wrote and produced himself."

The Diamonds Skiffle Group, St. Peter's Youth Club, Christmas 1961.

Author's note: *the Bellfields St. Peter's C. of E. Club did not attract anything like the same quality of acts as the Congo. My brother John and I were resident in Jacobs Well in the early 1960s. We formed some sort of basic "skiffle" group, with me on acoustic guitar and vocals and all the other three as percussionists (no amplification)! I am not quite sure what sort of sound we made, but we had a captive audience in the St. Peter's Church Youth Club. By*

THE VENUES

now we were definitely dressing to impress the girls. My friend, Russell Warden, and I spent much time in the cloakroom finalising the hairstyles and the shirt buttons (how much chest to expose!) before making an entrance. Happy days!

The Harvest Moon
The Moon was a prolific venue for groups of this period, although relatively short-lived between 1965 and '67. At the peak in '66 there was music there six nights of the week, plus Sunday afternoons.

The Harvest Moon was on the first floor of the Rodboro Buildings, constructed in 1900, for the rapidly expanding motor manufacturer Dennis and is said to be the world's first purpose-built car factory. It adjoins the bus station and the gyratory road system and in 1990 it was unused, in a poor state and demolition for further road widening

97

was a serious proposal. The building was, of course, preserved and is now home to one of J. D. Wetherspoon's super pubs on the ground and first floor with the Academy of Contemporary Music above. It was used for a variety of purposes over the years, until it fell into disuse in the 1980s.

The Moon was the home for the mods. This was a proto type of the modern night club which would be recognisable to today's youngsters. This was a late night venue and the more famous artists to play there included Eric Clapton and Gino Washington. But by 1967 The Harvest Moon was on the way out.

In May the Guildford and Godalming Times reported that:

"A youth arrested at The Harvest Moon Club and taken to Guildford Police Station for questioning regarding breaking and stealing offences was searched and found in unlawful possession of 22 tablets and a quantity of powder containing the drug amphetamine. There he asked police why they 'kept on at The Harvest Moon. It's not a bad place after all.'"

On 3rd June the same newspaper reported that:

"The Harvest Moon Club is closing down and next Saturday's dance will be its finale. The club, in Onslow Street, Guildford, has long been a controversial talking point, due to its association with drug peddling, and the owners give this as the reason for the closure.

A statement issued over the weekend begins: "The owners of The Harvest Moon Club have decided to close the club as from Sunday, June 4th. The reason for this is the prevalence of the soft drugs - pep pills - in the age group of the majority of the club members.

"The club was opened in February 1965 as a young people's recreational centre. Supervision was unobtrusive, but effective, and the club flourished.

"It was an experiment, which had of necessity to be commercially viable, and one which set out to provide something for a large section of the 16-22 age group who did not wish to be part of an organised youth movement, whether the youth club, church or service organisation.

"It is estimated that at least 40-50% of this age group in the Guildford area - some 5,000/6,000 people - are in this category.

"That it has failed, through a national problem, will no doubt cause relief and even satisfaction in some quarters. That there is a need for such a centre cannot be denied and to do so is to refuse to accept the facts.

"Over 100,000 young people have used the club in the last two years and whether we like it or not, young people are growing up quicker and are not prepared to be treated as their counterparts were 20 years ago, or even 10 years ago."

The statement continues: "Late parties - dances - call them what you will, are here to stay, and it might well be considered better for them to be in their own town than scattered along the south coast or up in London.

"Meanwhile, club members danced through last Saturday night, completely unaware of the closure. When newly opened, the club attracted star names such as Acker Bilk and Chris Barber. On Friday night, a blind Puerto Rican guitarist, José Feliciano, who is on his first tour of this country, will play the club's swan song.

"Giving evidence to a select committee of the House of Commons in April in connection with the Guildford Corporation Bill, Police Superintendent D. Tunn-Clarke said there was a considerable drug problem in Guildford and of 49 offences in the previous year all but 3 concerned people who had either been in or were going to The Harvest Moon Club.

"He said that the attitude of the management had been most helpful and they had invited the police to send officers in at any time they wished.

"The Corporation Bill, which is not expected to become law until the late summer, gives Guildford Town Council and the police stricter control on the licensing of clubs and bars which operate between 11 p.m. and 5 a.m. Such clubs will have to be registered annually and police and corporation officials will have powers of entry."

The drugs predominantly used were pep pills or amphetamines. Also, to some extent, the smoking of cannabis resin. The pep pills came in various grades, including "blues", "yellows" (dexodrin) and something horrendous called a "Black Bomber". The effect of all of these in varying degrees was to give tremendous energy, the ability to talk the hind leg off a donkey and suffer a serious hangover the next day.

Author's note: *the only time I was ever searched for drugs was outside The Harvest Moon, when I was asked by the police to remove my shoes (a common hiding place for drugs) and the only time in this period I took drugs was when my drink was spiked at the Civic Hall!*

With The Whiskey Ring, I was at one stage working five gigs a week, including in the NAAFI and The 4 'A's club in Aldershot, Civic Hall Guildford and Cranleigh Village Hall. A gig which particularly sticks in the mind for me was at The Harvest Moon where we were supporting Peter Green. Peter Green (later of Fleetwood Mac), like me, was only 19 years of age, yet an outstanding guitarist who had obviously, along the same lines as Eric Clapton, studied the blues and practised incessantly. He was a great guy and we chatted about groups and equipment. For our second set he suggested that I try out his new amplifier. I know that many of my contemporaries also have kind words to say about Peter.

It was around this time that I had my first sight of Eric Clapton. This was at The Harvest Moon. Clapton had already had considerable cult success with The Yardbirds and had recently been recruited to The John Mayall Blues Breakers. There were only a few of us in The Harvest Moon that night. We stood by the stage and were blown away partly by the sheer volume from Clapton's Gibson Les Paul guitar with the new high powered Marshall amplifier in overdrive. In fact,

THE VENUES

we thought he was too loud[1]. We had known The Blues Breakers as a band and we felt that this was a little bit over the top on Eric's part. We even slipped down the pub part the way through. We weren't to know that we were watching history in the making!

Apart from The Harvest Moon, another all-night club to be eventually closed down because of drugs was The Shore Line at Bognor, known as the first teenage hotel.

The Stoke Hotel

The Stoke Hotel is a large pub at the junction of Markenfield Road and A320 Stoke Road, close to the railway line and opposite The Kings Head (but not *the* King's Head in Quarry Street). It is the nearest pub to the Technical College and Art School and was used by some of the lecturers and students at lunchtime. It had a large function room where bands played. A particular gig to remember was the Art School party, where The Stormsville Shakers played. By 1967 the gigs were becoming less well attended and, being in a residential area, there were complaints from neighbours, eventually leading to a temporary close down following a Pink Floyd gig which included their mind expanding light show.

Jim Cook's Whisker Davis Blues Stormers were a regular support band at this venue, supporting Alexis Korner (one of the founders of the British blues boom) and Jimmy James and The Vagabonds. The Shakers' Manager, Chris Cassap, put on regular events there on Sunday nights.

---

[1] This was perhaps the start of the quest for volume. Ironically a little later in 1969, Eric is quoted as saying of Led Zeppelin "they were very loud - I thought it was unnecessarily loud. I really did like some of it, but a lot of it was just too much. They over-emphasised whatever point they were making, I thought."

GUILDFORD - THE ROCK'N'ROLL YEARS

Whisker Davies Blues Stormers, 1966
Above: from left to right:
Vin Godier – guitar, Jim Cook – bass guitar, Pete Newberry – drums (later founder of the Gin Mill Club),
Jim Luck – vocals, Whisker Davis – keyboards.

THE VENUES

Racks Close

The most unusual setting for an outdoor Sunday afternoon concert was the old quarry pit at Racks Close, not far from Quarry Street, featuring three top acts: Graham Bond Organisation; The Herd featuring Peter Frampton; and Gino Washington and The Ram Jam Band. Jim recalls that "the Mayor lived just above the quarry and put in an appearance to make sure all was well". Phillip Goodhand-Tait's recollections are of losing money as The Stormsville Shakers were the promoters of this ambitious undertaking.

The Tunsgate Club

In the early sixties, clubs in Guildford were few and far between. Gigs were mainly youth clubs and village halls and the occasional pub. The Tunsgate was the first club for live groups. It was on the first floor of the building fronting High Street, over Russell & Bromley's. It was run by one Tom Stredwick. It was a good old-fashioned club. The band set up at the south end, away from the High Street frontage. There were bar stools, a small seating area and dance floor.

This was not officially a late club, but the conventional 11 p.m. finish. At that time pubs in the Guildford area closed at 11 p.m. Fridays and Saturdays and 10.30 p.m. the rest of the week. The Tunsgate was a members' club and in the days of pre-24 hour pub drinking, this type of club was frequented by afternoon drinkers. In the late sixties it became Dronfields, the first "disco only" type nightclub in Guildford.

Norman Harris, a regular at the club, recalls that in the autumn of 1963 the dancing was so vigorous that the light fittings were knocked off the ceiling in Russell & Bromley shoe shop below. As a result, the club was not closed but they stopped having groups for a while so that the floor could be strengthened. Not to be deterred, manager Tom Stredwick hired The Stoke Hotel ballroom on Sunday afternoons and put on groups for Tunsgate members only, but no bar. By the end of

November, groups resumed at The Tunsgate.

Aldershot
Although some 10 miles to the west of Guildford and actually in Hampshire, Aldershot and Guildford have many links, including musical. Aldershot is well known as a garrison town. It had a number of entertainment centres, including at that time a Fourth Division Football Club and, on occasion, attracted punters from the Guildford area. In 1966, Jimi Hendrix played at the ABC Cinema, Aldershot.

In the early days of The Beatles, one of their agents, Sam Leach, tried to arrange a gig for them in London, but had to make do with The Queen's Hall, Aldershot, where he ran two shows. Due to a mix up with the local press, the gig was not advertised. London agents were invited but did not bother to turn up. He hired the hall from Bob Potter. They went round the local pubs and coffee clubs offering free admission, but only 18 people turned up. Sam Leach asked them to spread out, to make it look like a crowd. He says in "Follow the Mersey Beat Road" (publisher Eden Publications).

"After the performance I bought four crates of Watneys Brown Ale …… we had a football match on the dance floor - Liverpool v. Aldershot - we won of course."

As a result of the 1963 rock group competition (see Chapter 3), the Stormsville Shakers met their agent to be, Mike Burton. Amongst the gigs which he arranged for them was that well-known venue for Guildford groups, The NAAFI Club, Aldershot, where the fee at the time was £6.

Says Phillip Goodhand-Tait:

"The NAAFI Club was a dangerous place to perform. Soldiers in training or on leave heavily outnumbered females and on almost every evening there resulted in fights which embroiled the whole room until the Military Police broke them up. We became adept at defending our territory, the stage, from squaddies seeking our destruction, prodding them away with microphone stands. How we were never seriously injured I will never know, except that the stage was 6 ft. to 8 ft. above the dance floor, so we had a bit of an advantage. We always sought to retain the high ground."

Chapter 6
The Music Shops

Guildford girl, Betty Thornton, remembers searching the wave bands of her radio and, in particular, finding the American Forces network and discovering the great sounds of the likes of Johnny Cash and Ray Charles. She was steeped in the pop music of the late 1950s and early sixties. Her cousin was John Kelly of skiffle group fame - see chapter 1 of this book - and she started work selling records, record players and music in Collis Woods in North Street.

Author's note: *by the autumn of 1958, my pocket money allowed me to start buying records. The first record I ever bought was from Collis Woods and was "The Grand Coolie Dam" by Lonnie Donegan[1]. This had been released earlier in the year.*

My parents had an old radiogram, dating from the 1930s, which only played 78 rpm records. All their classical symphonies which they owned were made up of a series of 78s. In the late 50s most records were available in either 45 or 78 rpm format.

Betty must have been very familiar with this situation - punters asking for either the 78 rpm or 45 rpm version - depending on whether they had an old fashioned radiogram or a modern "record player".

Betty subsequently moved to Andrews in Quarry Street (in the same ownership as Collis Woods) and then, when it first opened, Barnes & Avis at the bottom of the High Street.

As one entered Barnes & Avis on the ground floor, one passed through all the vacuum cleaners, other electrical appliances and pianos

---

[1] Impressed to hear that Betty subsequently actually visited the Grand Coolie Dam.

THE MUSIC SHOPS

before reaching the other musical instruments and records. At that stage, the upper floor was devoted to classical music, but later the musical instruments moved to that floor.

The then high cost of electrical goods in comparison with modern times has been mentioned elsewhere in this book. A good example is the cost then of a 12" L.P. at 35/- (£1.75). That L.P. was probably the equivalent of about 12 hours work for the average teenager.

Betty Thornton with one of her heroes, Jerry Lee Lewis.

Barnes & Avis was a great place for band members and followers to meet on a Saturday morning, putting up posters for gigs, listening to records, etc. Betty even organised coach trips to London to see the American artists. She recalls seeing Eddie Cochran performing in

London on his 1960 tour.

"The curtains opened and he stood with his back to the audience. He turned round - wow, amazing - those blue eyes, and what a great guitarist."

In the early sixties Betty met and subsequently married Mark Ackerman, who became a reporter with The Surrey Advertiser and kicked off the "go-ahead generation" series.

One particular incident at the shop is remembered by Betty. Part of their business was hiring out pianos. Her assistant, Jim, was happy to tell her that they had made a hiring out at Kingston. Betty immediately realised that this was for the Kingston Jazz Cellar, where Jerry Lee Lewis was appearing that night. She went up to see the gig and, of course, Jerry was pumping the ivories in the usual manner, including with his feet! Surprisingly, the piano came back in one piece, although Barnes & Avis never got paid.

Betty emigrated with Mark in 1964 and returned to Guildford in the early 1970s. Her continued association with the music scene saw her marrying Dave Sherrington, ex of The Stormsville Shakers and their son, Daniel, playing sax in the Brighton area to this day.

Around 1961, Phillip Goodhand-Tait had become friendly with Betty Thornton when she was working in music shops in Guildford. Betty was kind enough to let Phill know when she had a record she thought might interest him. Some of these records were rarities, only one copy being available to the shop. She would let Phill listen to the record in the booth and take down the lyrics, without the actual need to buy the record. In 1973 he dedicated a song "Teenage Canteen" to Betty on one of his albums, which has the refrain -

"Teenage Canteen, who could ask for anything more
than meeting all your friends in a record booth
taking in the music surely was a food
when the teenage canteen was the record store."

THE MUSIC SHOPS

Phill says:

"In those days in the early sixties, it was usual for customers to ask to hear a vinyl single record before buying it. To ensure that the customer didn't make off with the disc, they were played on a turntable operated by the assistant behind the counter and the sound was heard through speakers in a booth. At busy times there could be half a dozen booths playing different singles and as many as 3 or 4 people gathered at each one, listening. Of course, the general idea was that the customer bought the disc once they were satisfied it was the right song/performance, etc. In our case that was never going to happen. We were skint. I was still at school.

"There were one or two special glass encased booths with turntables in them, in which trusted customers might be allowed to play a long playing disc (album) before buying. Betty allowed us into the special booth with an armful of the latest single releases, provided the coast was clear.

"Betty's co-assistant, Marie, knew shorthand and would take down the lyrics for us."

Phillip Goodhand-Tait and Dick Forcey of The Stormsville Shakers in the record booth at Barnes & Avis.

GUILDFORD - THE ROCK'N'ROLL YEARS

Dave Sherrington's first job at age 15 was at Andrews as a shop assistant, selling sheet music, pianos, guitars, violins and carrying out minor instrument repairs. He worked there until age 17 and then says Dave:

"The son of the manageress of Collis Woods was Doug Buchan, a guitarist. Both he and I were keen fans of Django Reinhardt and even had a small band playing that type of jazz. Doug mentioned to me that there was a series of films being shown at the National Film Theatre in London about Django. I was desperate to see these films and threw a sicky. I was waiting at Guildford station to catch the train to Waterloo, when who should be there but the manager of Andrews. 'I thought you were ill' says he. 'Yes I am on my way up to London to see a specialist' I replied. He was not taken in. So it was Django who got me the sack!"

Around the end of 1963 Ian Latimer of The Phantom Four left school and started work at Barnes & Avis, which in his words "was heaven". Like his father, he was a natural born salesman (and also like his father ended up in electrical sales - his father had worked at the wholesalers, Sun Electrics, in Ladymead). Merina Madeswick was in charge of the record department on the ground floor of Barnes & Avis at this stage and Ian, at the tender age of 16½ was "in charge" of the music department upstairs. He was "in charge" because he was the only person working there! All the local musicians used to come in on a Saturday morning and try out all the instruments. Ian and his brother, Andy, had a golden opportunity to experiment. Ian particularly remembers trying out the Hofner bass, although his first bass guitar was actually a Futurama. There was a coffee bar opposite the shop (The Continental) and a little later The Phantom Four's first demo appeared on the juke box of that shop (see chapter 9 for more of the Phantom Four).

♪♫

THE MUSIC SHOPS

Pete Anderton was born within the sound of Bow Bells at Blackfriars, London, in November 1946. His family later moved to outer London at Fulham, having first spent a few years in Battersea. Pete lived in Fulham from age 7, passed his 11 plus and went to Elliott Comprehensive School, which is just to the north of Putney Heath. This was a brand new comprehensive school, in the days before secondary schools were comprehensive and appears somewhat to have followed the pattern of George Abbot, Burpham, but on a larger scale. It had three sections, grammar, secondary modern and technical, with three classes in each section per year and therefore a total of nine classes per year.

Pete's father, Harry, was a detective sergeant in the CID in the Metropolitan Police. His first love, however, was playing the drums. Technically, policemen were not supposed to have a second income through running their own business. In practice, it appears to have been condoned. In addition to playing the West End hotels in a dance band, Harry played the Masonic gigs. It is therefore not beyond the bounds of possibility that Harry would have been recognised by some of the punters at some of these gigs. Playing in the dance band was not exactly a conflict of interest, but there could of course be times when Harry was called out to an emergency, could not make the gig, but being ever the professional, would provide a stand-in drummer.

The police flat in which the Anderton family lived was one of three in a block in Fulham. Fortuitously from Peter's point of view, in the next door house lived Jimmy Grant, one of the producers of "Saturday Club", a Saturday morning radio show from 10 a.m. till noon, being a weekly pop music programme, introduced by Brian Matthew and featuring leading groups and singers. New releases and listeners requests were also included.

In his role as producer, Jimmy Grant received all the records published, which after use as required on the BBC, were given to young Peter. Pete recalls receiving piles (possibly hundreds) of these every week. "Most of them were rubbish, but there were one or two hits."

The Harry Anderton Band 1947.

Around age 11, Pete was part of a skiffle group, playing a pair of bongos. From these he gradually moved onto drums and as young as age 13 was deputising for his dad with a pianist (Max Boyd from Putney) at a Sunday lunchtime pub gig in Cable Street in the east end.

Peter had two younger sisters, but neither they nor his mother were musicians. Pete's dad had the drums stored at the flat, but the only practice possible was on home made practice pads. Harry was into big band jazz, swing and not rock'n'roll by any means, but did not discourage Pete from following his ambitions in that direction.

The three streams within the grammar section of Elliot School were 'A', 'S' and 'H' (the streams of the other sections carried on with the lettering to spell the word 'Ashburton' - the estate on which the school was located). In year two, Peter was in the 'S' stream, but by year three had been moved up to the 'A' stream. One of his fellow pupils in

THE MUSIC SHOPS

that class was Peter Green, later of Fleetwood Mac. Peter Green had a brother several years older, Micky, who had a group, Micky Green and The Cannons. Pete Green himself by this stage was playing the guitar and became good mates with Pete Anderton. They even performed in a school concert together. Pete Anderton recalls Peter Green as a "lovely guy" with whom he virtually lost contact after Peter Green left school at the earliest opportunity in the fourth year.[1]

Previous Saturday boy and Harry Webber at the Hammersmith Music Store.

[1] The last time the two Peters met was when Peter Green played at GuilFest when Pete Anderton sponsored a stage and Peter Green was playing.

Around 1962-64, Pete Anderton was playing in a good rock band in the Putney area with gigs in the West End and Hammersmith and in 1962 Harry was posted to Hammersmith. In Hammersmith there was in Peter's words:

"A wonderful olde worlde music shop, King Street Music Store, run by one Harry Webber.

"Dad used to pop into the shop for bits and pieces, sticks, etc. and befriended Harry, who was a bit of a character and perhaps not always on the right side of the law. Nonetheless, the friendship was appreciated by both parties.

"Harry's Saturday boy had left. Harry was of the old school - violins, etc., and knew little about pop music. Dad suggested that I might make a good replacement for the Saturday boy.

"Although it was a tiny shop, the local musicians used to love coming in there to do a deal with Harry. I remember The Who, Georgie Fame and the BBC musicians from the Shepherds Bush studios coming in, as well as other rock and jazz musicians. Our great competitor was a shop up the road run by Mr. Friedman, which we called 'The Shiny Shop'.

"I used to work at the Music Store during the school holidays. I did the window dressing and I knew about drums. Harry Webber knew little about drums and regarded me as sharp enough to be sent off to the West End to meet the wholesalers and buy stock - cymbals, drums, etc. from the likes of Drum City Wholesalers. I did not drive, but Harry sent me off in a taxi! This was great. I got to know all the reps and wholesale managers. Harry taught me instrument repairs, including drum recovering. The great thing was I made so many contacts working on a Saturday with other musicians and as a result I was offered numerous gigs."

Peter was an excellent pupil during his first and second years at Elliott School, but by the time he reached the third year in his words he thought "this education must be a piece of cake", and stopped

THE MUSIC SHOPS

working. He used to bunk off for weeks at a time, including to the local snooker hall. As a result, he failed all his O- and A-levels, apart from art. Opening a music shop with his father began to look like a good idea.

In 1964 Harry Anderton was 49 years old, one year away from being able to retire from the police force. By now he was fed up with life in the force. He liked the look of the lifestyle which Harry Webber led, which he imagined consisted of little more than pottering around the shop. He decided he would like to set up his own music shop business.

Pete had a number of aunts on his mother's side, living in the Godalming area (his mother had been evacuated there during the war). Having made a fruitless search for premises in the London area, Pete and his dad therefore decided to look further afield and, knowing well the Guildford/Godalming area just down the A3 from Putney, they decided this would be a good place to set up. They did not own their own property and in order to raise the capital for the new venture, they had to sell the family car, the Ford Consul (although they had use of an old van), but more particularly sell the family record collection. Part of the capital was raised through a loan from one of Harry's old insurance buddies that he had met through the police force. There was a slight cushion and overlap in that Harry was not yet fully retired and indeed would receive a police pension when that time came and he was able to devote himself fully to the music shop. "Harry Webber, bless his cotton socks, provided us with some stock, and I knew all the reps who gave us some credit", says Pete.

Pete recalls finding their first premises at 18/20 Stoke Fields, which was then a greengrocers owned by a Mr. Mears.

Pete continues:

"Part of the attraction of this shop was that there was living accommodation, three bedrooms over, and behind the shop a sitting/dining room, kitchen and bathroom. Guildford was a one-horse town. I was a London boy. I had to get used to the slow pace. Our only competitor was Barnes & Avis. Local musicians also bought their equipment from Bells at Surbiton (mainly a mail order outfit). For some months I used to come down on the train from Putney every day to work on getting the shop ready. It needed completely gutting. There were rats nests, all sorts. We made our own blinds, we did everything. Dad was still in the police force until September '64, but used to come down at weekends to help. We slept on mattresses on the floor.

"Around this time I got my driving licence and started to commute down in the van rather than on the train. We were gearing up for an opening date of 6th June, 1964 and we duly met our own deadline."

On 3rd December, 1964, The West Surrey Outlook interviewed Pete Anderton. He is quoted as saying:

"So much cash is tied up in the beat group music business, that the big commercial concerns will ensure that the boom continues indefinitely. The standard of musicianship in the beat groups is improving. They are demanding better quality instruments. Local

THE MUSIC SHOPS

ANDERTON'S
Modern Music Centre

Guildford's largest stockists of Musical Merchandise

SPECIALISTS IN DRUMS AND ALL GROUP EQUIPMENT

18/20 STOKE FIELDS
GUILDFORD

PHONE 5928

An advertisement for Anderton's.

groups are now prepared to spend a thousand pounds to get the right sound. Anyone who doubts that there is a future in pop music should see the succession of schoolboys who come in here for their first jumbo guitar. We are also selling electric organs at £200 each and the piano is coming back into its own.

"All the well known local groups, including The Stormsville Shakers, The Primevals and The Nighthawks obtain their equipment here, and frequently make use of our repair service. We make everyone welcome, from the beginner to the professional musician.

Questioned on the possible effects of the new import tariff, Pete Anderton doubted whether it would affect trade. "Although 95% of our goods are imported from Japan and America, instrumentalists who require the best will be prepared to pay the extra."

Pete now says:

"Our timing was perfect. On a Saturday people were queuing up to get into the shop. The only problem was that we could not get enough stock, but fortunately, as I knew all the London wholesalers, I was able to exert some influence in getting them to divert stock from other

117

retailers to ourselves. We were not a big corporate like Barnes & Avis. We were therefore not hamstrung when it came to dealing with wholesalers. We could afford to slightly discount goods and we gave credit."

Peter and his father carried on playing in their respective bands, although gradually met musicians in the Guildford area through the shop. Harry then started his own dance band in the Guildford area, playing at local hotels and such venues as The Civic Hall and Peter joined Just Five, starting as a five piece but later as a seven piece - oddly still called Just Five!

Just Five on stage at Sunbury, 1965.

Just Five's manager was to become one Colin Beattie (later Mayor of Godalming). A lot of gigs were arranged, including as far afield as Cornwall. Colin's major achievement, however, was to effect an introduction to the Arthur Howes agency in London. This led to the university circuit, supporting Geno Washington and The Ram Jam Band.

The initial line up of Just Five was Pete Anderton (drums), Barry

THE MUSIC SHOPS

Wallace (vocals), Dave Holt (guitar/keyboards), Martin Dunsford (bass) and Geoff Dunsford (guitar). Barry was some years older than the rest of the group and married with children. He was from Godalming, the Dunsford brothers from East Horsley and Dave Holt from the Clandon area. The keyboard was the new Vox Continental organ.

The original Just Five. Barry Wallace, Martin Dunsford, Geoff Dunsford, Pete Anderton, Dave Holt.

Initially, the sound was the standard Chuck Berry fare, but this soon changed to a more soul based sound. The line up was sometimes supplemented with saxes before it became a permanent seven piece. Bob Webb from Wimbledon, some years older than the rest, played sax. They had another sax player, but for the tours they brought in Pete King, a well established session saxophonist. Barry the singer had a great voice in the Tom Jones style, well suited to R & B and soul. A record was made at the R. G. Jones Studio in Morden, initially as a demo but actually released. Around this time the two Dunsford brothers changed roles, with Martin taking up the bass and Geoff the guitar. Early in 1966 The Surrey Advertiser reports as follows.

"This year - although it is only just over a month old - has seen an upsurge in the fortunes of the Godalming based group, Just Five.

"A tour with American girl singer, Fontella Bass, has been completed and they are about to start on another tour with Gene Pitney and Len Barry, with the added prospect of a prolonged Italian trip.

"The group became fully professional on January 1st, when it signed up with Arthur Howes agency.

"This brought it a 16-day tour with Fontella Bass - recorder of "Rescue Me" and "Recovery" - which included a date at The Flamingo.

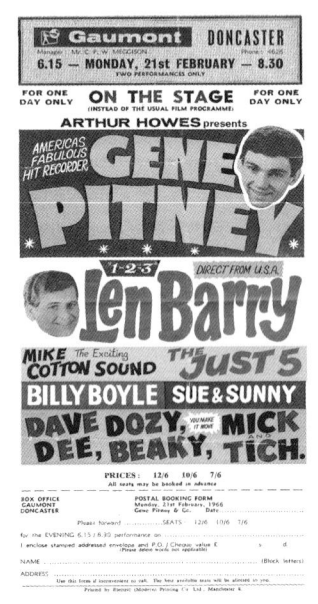

"But for Fontella's illness, it would have backed her on Saturday Club and would have also played at The Marquee[1].

---

[1] In fact that they did actually play at The Marquee.

THE MUSIC SHOPS

"When the tour was completed, Fontella paid the group the tribute of saying she would have liked to take it back to the States with her as her permanent backing group.

"Last week the group had a rest and its next big date is February 12th, when it begins its second national tour of one nighters with Gene Pitney and Len Barry."

Fontella Bass was over from the U.S.A. with her husband, a trumpeter. This was her inaugural tour of the U.K. and "Rescue Me" was number 1 in the charts. The tour took in all the top U.K. clubs.

The Gene Pitney/Len Barry tour was a package tour. They all travelled on a coach and as Pete recalls: "Gene used to sit up front with his bottle of scotch. There were no drugs on that tour. What put me off drugs was playing with some of the top jazz and blues musicians and seeing the effects which heroin could have."

They performed in Odeon cinemas, including that in Guildford. Pete remembers it well, the adrenaline running, the audience girls screaming. Included on the tour were in Pete's words "two gorgeous girls from the Camberley area of Surrey, Sue and Sunny".

The Gene Pitney tour brochure reviews Sue and Sunny in the following terms:

"Until Sunny was ten, the family lived in Stockport, Cheshire, but then they moved to Camberley, Surrey. At age ten Sunny entered herself into a local talent contest and later brought her sister in on the act. Their father looks after the business and the girls started appearing in ballrooms and cabarets up and down the country. Their recording career followed and they made a number of television appearances, including on Ready, 'Steady, Go'.

"Sue and Sunny's real names are Yvonne and Heather Weetman. Yvonne is Sue and Heather is Sunny."

Len Barry's hit "One, Two, Three" was current. Just Five provided the backing for Len Barry and also in their own right opened the second half of the show. Dave, Dee, Dozy, Beaky, Mick and

121

Titch were also on this tour. In reviewing the performance at the

Just Five became seven!

Cheltenham Odeon, June Southworth reported:

"I watched the second house from out front. Just Five ... who are seven ... opened the show wearing suits, honking saxes. Sue and Sunny, sisters from Surrey, are next on. They are Tamla Motownish and very exciting.

"Len Barry bounces on stage, looking very big and cuddly. Backing him are Just Five and Sue and Sunny, and they get a big blues feel going."

Mr. and Mrs. Harry Anderton.

THE MUSIC SHOPS

Turning pro had perhaps proved a step too far for one or two members of the band, including Pete. It meant that his dad, Harry, was left to manage the shop on his own. Pete felt he had to make a choice and gig on a more restricted basis, for example, teaming up with Geoff Andrews, formerly of The Primevals, on bass and Tony Boast on guitar to form The Other Two Thousand. However, in January 1968 disaster struck. One of Pete's great interests was horse riding and in that month he had a bad accident from which it took him a year to fully recover. He could not drum during that period, but could in his words "hobble around the shop".

The timing of the accident was unfortunate to say the least. The existing shop was bursting at the seams and the decision had been made to move to new premises at 91 Haydon Place. This was taken over from A. E. Boyman & Sons. At this stage the York Road extension did not exist. Now the new premises are to the south of York Road. After the subsequent move of Andertons to 58/59 Woodbridge Road in 1991, the premises at 91 Haydon Place for a while became Guildford's Academy of Contemporary Music.

This academy is an interesting aside to this story. Phil Brookes, a guitarist and teacher, had a vision of starting a music school in the field of rock, but had no business acumen or money. Pete Anderton through his shop and contacts had the premises and experience and was able to gain credit. The academy started in the Haydon Place premises in 1995. Pete says

"Phil's vision was to teach kids to play rock'n'roll in an exciting way and in a way in which they wanted to learn, but to a class of 25 or 30. Economically this made sense. Prior to that kids wanting to learn the guitar had to have individual tuition, which was expensive for them, but did not provide the tutor with much remuneration.

"We had to overcome the generally held view that rock'n'roll was not proper music. In our view this was nonsense. Rock'n'roll had a 40 year history by now.

"Eventually, Phil's documented teaching system was recognised by the powers that be. This was a proper accredited educational framework and exam system and then we got some central government funding.

"Around 2000 we moved in to the Rodboro building. This followed years of negotiation, planning and conversion. We were in competition with the Guildford School of Acting for the premises, which were owned by the Borough Council. I had put a huge amount of my own money on the line for this venture. It had to work.

"One of the problems we had was that Wetherspoons' lease precluded them from having live music. Accordingly, no sound could transmit from the school of music into their premises. We had the whole of the top floor and most of the middle floor. Wetherspoons had the ground floor and part of the middle floor. A great deal of our investment went into engineers fees for designing and producing sound proofing.

"The initial idea for a concrete floating floor proved too heavy for

THE MUSIC SHOPS

the foundations. I returned from holiday to be told that the scheme was therefore dead in the water. By this time, I was too heavily involved to give up. We started from scratch again and employed some excellent acoustic specialists to produce the sound proofing system. I had to sign a guarantee to the Council that the sound would not transmit to Wetherspoons. We had to commit to accepting 150 students 18 months ahead without, at this stage, any guarantee that we could meet the deadline. Of course, we did meet the deadline, but the stress was enormous.

"A further aside is that Bruce Dickinson, one of my managers, broke away and formed the Brighton Institute of Modern Music. For my part in 2007 I wanted to retire and managed to negotiate the sale of my interest to Phil."

Talking of the current Academy of Contemporary Music, it is interesting to compare the situation in the 1960s with that in the 2000s. Rock music has moved into the main stream. It is now a subject worthy of serious study. Many of the young current musicians are technically brilliant. This compares with the situation in the sixties where we were all self-taught. To learn a song involved painstakingly listening to a record in stages, jotting down the words as best one could hear them, and working out the chords. Very little pop music was available in written form and, in any event, it was certainly more important to have a feel for the music than be able to read music. The words and music to many tracks are now available via the internet. Many musicians now write their own music and the internet is also a boon to them with regard to putting their name about via MySpace, web cams, etc. The downside of the current situation is the lack of paid live gigs available to groups.

Not everyone is enamoured with the idea of the formalised approach to rock music tuition. Dave Sherrington (although he had been taught the clarinet) was a self-taught sax player. When asked if he would give lessons on the sax, his advice is "Yes, I will give you one lesson. Buy the best sax you can afford. Listen to as much sax music as you can and never stop practicing. I will not cater for your fantasies or dreams. My mother said to me - music has chosen you, you have not chosen music."

Andertons has always been a family run business. It is still going strong in Woodbridge Road, now run by Pete's son, Lee, and in 2004 celebrated 40 years of trading.

Chapter 7
'63 - '65 The Peak for the Beat Groups

Many of the groups in the Guildford area at this time were working a number of nights of the week and much of the work came through the agencies, who took 10% of the fee for arranging the work. Some groups also had managers who might or might not make a further deduction. Probably the biggest agency in south west Surrey in the 1960s was the Bob Potter Organisation, who signed The Age Beaters. Mick Douglas ran an agency in the Guildford area with Lionel Webb, known as DWG Entertainments. They obtained gigs for various Guildford groups, including The Primevals and The Phantom Four.

The Surrey Outlook reported in November 1964 as follows:

"Three young men who plan to revolutionise pop group entertainment in Guildford are attracting large numbers of teenagers to their promotions after only one year in business.

"The DWG Entertainments Agency of Guildford was formed in January this year by three local friends, Michael Douglas, Lionel Webb and Michael Gurney. The most experienced of the trio is Mr. Douglas, who is a professional guitarist.

"The DWG Agency has flourished in the past year, dealing mainly in semi-professional groups.

"The biggest event to date was booking The Undertakers (now known as The Takers) for The Angel Hotel, Godalming, in May."

It has been said that Bob Potter had the knack of hiring a group well in advance, at a relatively modest fee, only for that group to be at number 1 by the time the booking came round, but for the fee to have been fixed by contract. Bob ran The Atlanta Ballroom in Woking and from the seventies until the present day The Lakeside Country Club.

127

GUILDFORD - THE ROCK'N'ROLL YEARS

The Bumblies gained a residency at The Crown in Camberley every Sunday. This was next to The Agincourt Ballroom, run by Bob Potter. Unfortunately from Bob's point of view, The Bumblies popularity was such that they were drawing people away from The Agincourt and into The Crown. According to Terry Ward "this situation came to an end when one Sunday evening some hoodlums entered The Crown and wrecked the joint, after which there were no more gigs at The Crown."

♪♪

One group from the Guildford area was The Vibros. The Surrey Advertiser in November 1964 reported:

"Appearances on television and at The Prince of Wales Theatre, London, are already among the achievements of a group based in Normandy, who have only been in existence for ten months.

'63-'65 THE PEAK FOR THE BEAT GROUPS

"The group is The Vibros - four boys and a girl. The line up is Phil Halslem (17), rhythm guitar, John Obee (20), lead guitar, Bill Lowe (23), drums, John Eckett (21), bass guitar and his sister, Pam Eckett (18) who takes care of most of the vocals.

"They have enjoyed considerable success playing dates all over the south of England, whilst still on a semi-professional basis.

"Their Prince of Wales performance came when they won their way through to the final of a national beat competition. Of the 600 groups that entered, The Vibros got through to the last eleven.

"Among the groups with whom The Vibros have appeared are The Hollies, The Zombies and Brian Poole and The Tremeloes.

"Among the local dates they have played are The Guildford Civic Hall, The Guildford Plaza and Godalming Youth Centre."

♫♫

Another band from the early sixties, albeit relatively short-lived, was The Kai B's. A report in The Surrey Outlook of 1963 suggested that this was Guildford's loudest group. They had recently supported The Stormsville Shakers at The Wooden Bridge. The line up comprised Raymond Wallis (lead and vocals), Jerry Bowers (drums), Malcolm Denyer (rhythm and lead vocals), Steve Backhurst (bass and vocals), Mick Backhurst (manager and driver). The two Backhurst brothers worked at the plastic coatings factory where the group practiced twice weekly, where Ricky and The Rhythmics also practiced.

Unfortunately and inevitably there will be omissions of some who played a part in the sixties Guildford scene. Kevin and Trevor Finbow, Max Bevan and Mick Swears to name but a few were to some extent involved.

The Road Runners was a band operating in the mid-sixties and personnel included Roger Newman on guitar and Ryan Cheeseman on vocals. Yet another of the many local bands was The Smoke

The Kai B's: L - R. Steve Backhurst, Jerry Bowers, Michael Backhurst, Malcolm Denyer, Raymond Wallace.

Stakks. They appeared at the Arts School Christmas Party, supporting Rupert. The Surrey Advertiser reports their manager as being John Hewins and identifies the personnel of the group only by their Christian names as being Fred (19) on drums, Peter (20) on rhythm guitar, Jeff (18) on bass guitar, Roger (17) on lead guitar, Will (17) on harmonica and Tony (19) vocals.[1] They are reported as being greatly influenced by Sonny Boy Williamson and Jim Reed and having a bright future in the R & B world.

♪♫

Bert Curtis, who became the drummer in The Age Beaters, started in Guildford's Leopard Spots skiffle group, dealt with in the opening chapter of this book. Following this he played with The Sparklers, a piano, drums, clarinet and piano accordion quartet.

---

[1] Author's note: Tony was for a short while the singer with the Weysiders - see chapter 10.

'63-'65 THE PEAK FOR THE BEAT GROUPS

The line up of The Age Beaters was in 1964, Dave Everson, 21 (lead guitarist and vocalist), Pete Cannon, 18 (rhythm guitar), Alan Hatswell, 18 (bass guitar), Bert Curtis, 21 (drums), Bruce Bunker, 19 (manager). At a later stage, Dick Forcey replaced Bert on drums. Alan Hatswell, incidentally, had already played on the same bill as Cliff

131

Richard to an audience of 2,000. The Age Beaters were soon playing regularly at The Kingston Jazz Cellar, The Plaza, The Civic Hall, The Charlotteville Youth Club and The Tunsgate Club. Top spot in their act was when the group's manager did his Jack the Ripper act, dressed in top hat and cloak, in which he was carried on to the stage in a coffin from which he leapt with an unearthly shriek, his face covered in talcum powder! The group posed with Bruce in the coffin at St. Catherine's for a photographic session. According to the Surrey Advertiser at the time the police were called as onlookers thought that a black magic session was in progress!

The Age Beaters were one of the first groups to play at The Civic Hall and they played in the interval breaks of the then Big Band Palais Nights of Chris Allen. Chris announced them as a novelty rock'n'roll

'63-'65 THE PEAK FOR THE BEAT GROUPS

band, ending with the statement "the music won't last".

Dave Everson later formed The Dave Everson All Stars, whose members included Frank Ayling. It was during one of this group's gigs at the Civic Hall that Dave was nearly electrocuted. In Frank's own words

"Our first gig was at The Civic Hall. At the start of the show I got an electric shock from one of the microphones and I told Dave about it, but he said that will be OK. It was when the PA systems were all valve high voltage stuff and sometimes you would get a bad earth. Well, about half way into a song backing Rip Van Winkle, he had an act where he used to chop up a dummy of a girl with an axe. The dummy was filled with pig's blood or something. It was pretty bad. Anyway, Rip was swinging his axe when I looked across to Dave who was sort of hovering at a funny angle and shaking violently as he was being electrocuted. The crowd in the packed house thought it was part of the act and were cheering him on. Our back-up singer tried to get the guitar off him, but was thrown across the stage. In the end, someone turned the power off and they called an ambulance. He spent some time in hospital, the strings had burnt his fingers very badly. There were a lot of girls who fainted. Dave's wife was in the crowd and she was very shook up."

Dave Everson started playing the guitar in the 1950s and then moved to Australia for a short while, where he backed such luminaries as Bobby Vee and Cliff Richard. It was on his return from Australia in 1963 that he formed The Age Beaters.

Bruce Bunker, manager of The Age Beaters, also managed The Bumblies before Jonathan King.

Norman Harris was also a musician on the Guildford sixties music scene. His first group rehearsed at The Charlotteville Youth Club where he began on drums but later switched to piano. He was replaced by Ken Richards on drums. Two members of this group were Peter Cannon and Alan Hatswell (both later of The Age Beaters).

The Age Beaters

l - r: Dave Everson, Pete Cannon, Alan Hatswell and Bert Curtis

Bruce Bunker found Dave Everson and Bert Curtis and the five of them formed The Age Beaters. However, Norman left due to health problems before they started gigging.

Norman also sang on a part-time basis with various groups, including Peter Arthur (aka Ricky Clayton of The Rhythmics) at The Tunsgate Club. At this stage the group was called Nite Sounds, but later this changed to Sticks 'n' Stones. Norman did further scratch gigs on piano with Dave Everson with a varying line up and also played drums with The Age Beaters when Bert Curtis was not available. Groups with whom Norman appeared on a temporary basis included The Leeways.

♫♫

Other groups of this era included Ad Finitum (whose singer was Hughie Webb and drummer John Shepherd), The Oscillators and later Dick Middleton's The Bulldog Clip Rubber Band, whose name changed to Catwalk. Also the Cuttaways or Cutaways (the latter featuring Ian Jelfs, later of the Shakers and Circus) on the guitar. In addition, solo artist Steve Perry.

'63-'65 THE PEAK FOR THE BEAT GROUPS

The Cutaways.

The Cutaways perhaps deserve some special mention. The Guildford and Godalming Times of 3rd July, 1964, reported on the "Big Beat Festival", held at The Civic Hall the previous Sunday.

"Fresh from recent success in other beat competitions, The Primevals only managed to finish in the final six in this competition. Local honours this time went to a Godalming group, Paul and The Cutaways, who finished second.

"Judging in the earlier rounds was done by machine, which recorded audience reaction. Later the judging was performed by a panel, who decided that because of the distorted sound The Cutaways should lose points but otherwise might have finished first.

"All the groups used the same equipment supplied by Barnes & Avis.

"The winners were not a local group. They were The Silhouettes from Hastings, featuring a 16-year-old female vocalist. The Cutaways for finishing second received a cheque for £30.

"About 800 teenagers watched the eight hour long final, for which 14 groups had been chosen out of a total entry of nearly 300.

"The groups all performed during the afternoon; out of these, six were chosen to appear in the final in the evening. The Classics from Woking finished third.

"Although The Primevals, playing on their home ground, had an audible contingent of fans, they were overshadowed by The Cutaways' supporters who gathered at the foot of the stage, dancing and waving more banners.

"The group says that the main influence on the type of music they play has been Chuck Berry, of whom the boys are all great fans, and also possibly The Rolling Stones, although they are not prepared to grow their hair to Stone length.

"Outside of the Godalming area The Cutaways have played in London for private functions and are hoping to put their van to greater use for playing dates further afield.

"Quite naturally, the boys would like to become professionals eventually and feel they will be ready for this in about a year's time.

"Three of them have jobs at the moment, but they would be prepared to give up these if the opportunity comes for them to go pro. They are hoping to make a demonstration disc in the near future."

The Cutaways line up at this stage was Ian Jelfs, aged 15, from Farncombe, who had been playing almost as long as he had been able to hold the guitar. On bass guitar was Mick Dam from New Haw, aged 18. There was no rhythm guitarist, it being said that the sound was so solid they did not need one. The other members of the group were Paul Love, a 16-year-old vocalist with a surprising range, and his brother, Tony, aged 20, on the drums.

They were said to be the first group in the Guildford area to have a fan club, which was run by 15-year-old Linda Stocking of Milford, at which stage they had 80 members.

The Cutaways.

♪♫

The Surrey Advertiser also reported around this time regarding Simon and The Surreys.

"A group, whose name you'll be hearing quite often in the future, is Simon and The Surreys. 19-year-old leader and vocalist is Simon Brook of Walton-on-the-Hill, bass player is Terry (19) from Farnham, 18-year-old Ken Richards of Burpham is the drummer and Pete Hawkins (20) of Frensham Vale is the lead guitarist.

"The group, which is semi-professional, has been together for about 3 months and has played at dance halls and youth clubs up and down Surrey.

"They are gradually building up a following, especially in the London suburbs. Their biggest thrill so far has been playing at the

GUILDFORD - THE ROCK'N'ROLL YEARS

London Flamingo Club and the Brixton Granada.

"The two boys from the Guildford area, Terry and Ken, have both given up their jobs to devote more time to the group.

"Spokesman Simon told me: 'The group don't play strict beat music or rhythm and blues. We have a distinct sound of our own. We are a stage group and want to be seen.' "

Simon and The Surreys.

l - r: Ken Richards, Peter Hawkins, Terry Hutchins and Simon Brook.

♪♫

The Astolats reached the finals of the Great Britain Beat Contest, sponsored by Pember Enterprises Limited. They won the regional heat at the Agincourt Ballroom, Camberley and represented the south east in the finals at Dunstable. The members of the group were Paul Foster, lead guitar; Paul Cooper, bass guitar; John Campbell, rhythm guitar; Colin Kings, vocals and Tony Tidy, drums.

'63-'65 THE PEAK FOR THE BEAT GROUPS

The Astolats

♪♫

Another group from this period was The Sapphires (sometimes known as Johnny and The Sapphires). They rehearsed at Milford Village Hall. The line up comprised Johnny Cooper (vocals), Tony Bishop (lead guitar), John Walters (rhythm guitar), Bob Stratford (bass guitar) and Ken Ford (drums). Johnny had previously sung with The Mustangs (later to become The Bumblies). Their manager was Peter Ford. They appeared at The Plaza and The Rex Cinema, Haslemere.

GUILDFORD - THE ROCK'N'ROLL YEARS

Johnny and The Sapphires.

Also featuring in the Guildford area around this period were The Roadrunners with Ossie and Roger Newman on guitars, Ryan Cheeseman on vocals, Dave Dennis on bass and Victor from Woking on the drums. This band was going from around 1965 to '68 and played at such venues as The Harvest Moon.

♪♪

Ricky and The Secrets were a well-known group from Bellfields Estate. The lead guitarist was Chris Ball. He was born in 1946 and his family moved to Guildford in 1950, for his father to work at the newly established Ministry of Agriculture, Fisheries and Food.

140

'63-'65 THE PEAK FOR THE BEAT GROUPS

The Secrets, October 1963. L - R. Chris Ball, Ricky, Alan Bridle, Dave Phillips and Geoff Miles.

In the late summer of 1963, Chris, along with pals Dave Phillips and Alan Bridle, bumped into a bass player named Geoff Miles and the singer, Ricky Sharon (real name Ricky Loseley). By that time Chris had been playing the guitar for a year or two, initially at his school (Northmead). They rehearsed a couple of times a week at the Congo Youth Club before gigging under the name of Ricky and The Secrets. In the words of Chris Ball:

"The all important uniforms consisted of waistcoats, collar and tie, smart trousers and Angelo and Davide Cuban-heeled boots (which I sent away for - some trendy place in London). The waistcoats had been made by one of our mums.

"Equipment wise, Dave Phillips and myself played twin pick up Rosetti Air Stream II solid body electric guitars, I owned a 15 watt Selmer amp, Dave had a Watkins amplifier and Geoff Miles played an Air Stream bass through a Wem amplifier. We had a Selmer PA."

Geoff was the group's leader, who knew the right people to contact, and arranged gigs for the many local dances and at the clubs, including The Harvest Moon, Dronfields and Boxers.

l - r: Chris Ball (lead guitar), Ivan Moonsey (rhythm guitar), Peter Anderton (drums - standing in for Alan Bridle), Richard Loseley (vocalist) and Geoffrey Miles (bass guitar).

The Secrets got involved in appearing in a TV episode of a religious programme called The Sunday Break, fronted by Richard Lindley. This was in 1964 and the venue chosen for the programme was The Congo Club, Bellfields. Part of the programme featured a piece about a modern nativity play in a youth club and The Secrets were playing in the background. Just Alan Bridle's luck to be in hospital at the time and he was replaced by Pete Anderton. The pictured line up with Pete also appeared in the Surrey Advertiser. By this time the line up had also changed in that Dave Phillips had been replaced by Ivan Moonsey and the equipment had been upgraded. The Surrey Advertiser of 1964 reported as follows:

"The television appearance came about through the group's

'63-'65 THE PEAK FOR THE BEAT GROUPS

connection with Stoke Hill Congregational Youth Club.

"They played for the club's winning entry in the local drama festival and the leader, John Handby, wrote a second short episode which he submitted to the producer of "Sunday Break".

"He was fortunate as the piece he wrote fitted in with an idea the producer was working on. A beat group is needed and The Secrets fit the bill, playing 'Walking The Dog' and the background music, together with an original number written themselves. Ricky has already put pen to paper and come up with a number of songs which the group now feature in their act.

"The Secrets have found themselves a manager in Ken Brewer of The Plaza and Brian Simmons. Through them they got the chance to make a recording at Bob Potter's studio, which was 'Walking The Dog'. The group brought their tape away from the studio, but the master tape was left there and when a director of Radio Caroline listened to what had been recorded during the week, he chose The Secrets number as the best of the batch. As a result, it was played many times on Radio Caroline and Pete Murray gave it an airing on Radio Luxembourg.

"The Secrets will be returning to the studio in a week's time when they are to make another disc. This time it will be an EP. Brian Simmons is to take this round the promoters in the Bognor Regis and Worthing area in the hope of getting the group some dates there.

"Ricky has put pen to paper on several occasions and come up with new numbers that the group now feature in their act, including 'I Want Me A Woman' and 'Baby, What You Trying To Do?' "

Chris says:

"Another slightly bizarre episode I remember clearly was that some cinemas had a part of the stage that could be lowered and then brought up again, usually with the house organist appearing as if by magic and then playing between the films. Of course, the massive popularity of pop music at the time prompted theatre managers to use groups

GUILDFORD - THE ROCK'N'ROLL YEARS

The Secrets and members of Bellfields Congregational Youth Club ('The Congo').

instead of an organist to entertain the audience. The Rex Cinema in Haslemere (now long gone) was the one I remember the most. We didn't get paid, but we all (including girlfriends) got to watch the films for nothing!"

By this stage The Secrets were rehearsing at The Plaza, where they once played on the same bill as Little Eva at the height of her fame. Chris also remembers seeing a number of groups at The Plaza, including The Yardbirds with Eric Clapton and The Stones. He was particularly impressed by Keith Richards playing. Later that year The Secrets played on the same bill as Wayne Fontana and The Mindbenders at Esher Town Hall.

Chris Ball was approached by Mick Douglas in the mid-sixties with a view to going to Hamburg and playing there, but he was ensconced in a 7 year printing apprenticeship and his mum and dad were dead against it and so he never took up the offer.

"Even to this day, once in a blue moon I think about it, what would have happened if I had gone ….? But it's the fact that I didn't that still trips across my mind.

"By 1966 I knew I wasn't going to be a star, though I still played, the most notable being a year with a group called Finders Keepers from the Richmond/ Hersham area. I later played in the Cliff Carlton Band all over the south of England, including a show opened by Diana Dors. Those 20 years on the boards I wouldn't have missed for the world and count myself lucky enough to have been involved in just a small part of it all - the beat era."

♫♫

A band which was influential in Guildford in the early sixties, but about which little information is now available, was Hogsnort Rupert. The leader and singer is now based in Vancouver. Kirk Riddle recalls first having seen them in the early sixties at Merrow Village Hall at about the same time that The Shakers played there. Rupert's real name was Robert McGrath and at that stage the line up included on sax Greg McGregor (later of The Shakers).

They were partly made up of students from Farnham Art College, including Robert himself and, according to Kirk, their music was certainly more "way out" than that of The Shakers, being based on what Kirk describes as "New Orleans rock-n-roll" rather than the Chuck Berry type white man's rock'n'roll that The Shakers were playing.

A little later, in 1964, the Surrey Advertiser reported

"After an absence of about a year, Hogsnort Rupert, with his reformed band, returned to Guildford last week when he played at The Wooden Bridge Hotel.

"Rupert used to be a favourite on the Guildford scene, but disappeared last October when the band moved into London. Since then they have disbanded and Rupert concentrated on the promoting side of the business.

"The reformed band has been together some two months now. Although most of them come from around the Windsor area, they hope to be doing a lot more work in the Guildford area.

"Rupert, who has played such places as London's mod night spot 'The Discotheque', said that he got his name because some people think he laughs like a pig.

"The line-up of the band is Rupert, vocals; Rod Jones, electric piano; Brian Chambers, lead guitar; Dave Brown, bass guitar; Roland Vaughan, tenor sax; Johnny Clayton, tenor and bass sax; and John Constantine, drums.

"On Thursday night they gave out with some of the best Motown music heard on this side of the Atlantic. The gutteral of Rupert is supplemented by the deeper resonance of the band playing as a unit.

"When they split up into solos they have the scope to get greater variation on the theme and so provide a more interesting interpretation.

"The promoters, DWG Entertainments, hope to hold a session regularly every Thursday at The Wooden Bridge.

"Fans will be able to see them in action before that, however, as Rupert is appearing at The Civic Hall in October, supported by The Primevals."

There is a link between Hog Snort, art schools and that well known Guildfordian John Renbourn.

John Renbourn, born in London 1944, was a pupil at Pewley School, Guildford and George Abbot School. This was in 1964. Two years later he was playing folk music in Soho, where he met other musicians including Paul Simon, Davy Graham and Burt Jansch. At school he took music lessons and at the same time sat his grade exams on classical guitar at the Guildhall. On his web site, John says:

"The classical guitar studies helped a lot in the transition to steel string finger picking styles.

'63-'65 THE PEAK FOR THE BEAT GROUPS

"In Britain in the late fifties the musical craze was for skiffle, an amalgam of American folk, blues, blue grass and jug band styles. The big hit was 'Freight Train', which drew attention to Elizabeth Cotten's original, as well as to the work of such musicians as Leadbelly, Jessie Fuller, Josh White and Big Bill Broonzy. These players all came over to England and their guitar styles left a strong impression on a generation of young skifflers. As I left school I went hitch-hiking, and met up with others trying to play like them. Mac McLeod, Gerry Lockran, Mick Softely and Wizz Jones were already on the way, and we were all in awe of Davy Graham.

"In the early sixties I attended Kingston College of Art fairly frequently. The art school seemed to be turning out more musicians than artists at the time. The Yardbirds were at Kingston, as were Eric Clapton and Sandy Denny. The R & B craze had replaced skiffle and the best band was considered to Alexis Korner's Blues Incorporated.

"I played in an art school R & B band for a while, Hogs Snort Rupert's famous Porkestra, using a borrowed electric guitar. I found that some of the band's riffs sounded interesting played finger style on an acoustic guitar. Pieces like 'The Wildest Pig In Captivity' came out of that.

"Around 1963/64 I ran in to Burt Jansch."

After various experimental line-ups, Pentangle was formed. The first recording "The Pentangle" was picked up by Warner Brothers in America and things started happening fast. They toured America in 1968 playing prestigious gigs like Carnegie Hall and The Newport Folk Festival.

When there was a brief falling out between Phillip Goodhand-Tait and the rest of The Shakers, Rupert was actually auditioned in Shalford Village Hall as a possible replacement. According to Dave Sherrington:

"He was a great character both on and off the stage, but his singing was barely passable compared with Phill's and when told that the next gig was in Newcastle his reply was 'Bugger that - that's a light year away' - and that was the end of that."

On that note from Dave and Rupert - two great characters of the period - we shall move on.

CHAPTER 8
MORE VENUES AND LIFESTYLES

Godalming

Doreen Pettifer, the John Mayall Fan Club Secretary, wrote in her newsletter around the turn of 1968:

"Good news for fans in this area. The Angel Hotel in Godalming will on January 14th open as a blues club. The band booked for the opening is Dr. Brown's Gospel Medicine and it is also hoped that Tony (Duster) Bennet will be able to come along."

The very successful Gin Mill Club at Godalming's Angel pub was run by Pete Newberry. Jim Cook recalls:

"R & B had become less popular, but was about to return in a second wave and bigger than ever. I played bass regularly in The Spirit Level as support band to many great groups there, including Fleetwood Mac. They asked the two saxophone players from Spirit Level to play with them on their imminent recording session, which became their L.P. 'Mr. Wonderful'.

"Peter Green listened to an open reel recording I made of one of their performances at the club and said that it had a great atmosphere that they could not capture on their recordings. He gave me his address and asked me to send him a copy. Unfortunately, my recorder screwed up the tape and I didn't get back in touch!

"The Gin Mill Club hosted Jethro Tull, Free, Genesis, Fleetwood Mac, Chicken Shack, Champion Jack Dupre, Duster Bennet and Savoy Brown. It had a tremendous atmosphere and Fleetwood Mac returned several times after their hit record because they loved playing there. Jethro Tull were a little more precious and nearly didn't play as the club was so small."

Martin Celmins in his book "Duster Bennet - Jumping At Shadows" (the authorised biography published by Jet Martin, August 2007) quotes Tony "Duster" Bennet in an interview with Melody Maker's Jeremy Gilbert in late 1969 on how he got into the music business full time during 1967.

"I couldn't really see myself as a musician until I met Pete Newberry who runs The Angel and he persuaded me to do a gig. The only person I knew at Godalming was Pete."

Duster Bennet's one man band was reviewed in May 1967 by The Surrey Advertiser as part of the Godalming Blues Concert. The Graham Bond Organisation was headlining but, according to a reviewer, Tony Bennet stole the show.

"For the first part of his act, Tony was accompanied by Anthony Topham on guitar and Tony Mills on jug, calling themselves The Georgia Skin Boys. Anthony Topham's country style guitar blended in particularly well with Tony's fast chord work."

Martin Celmin's book records the following:

"Early in 1969 Duster Bennet decided to record a live album. The date and place was set: 17th April at a Duster Bennet stronghold - The Angel Hotel in Godalming, Surrey. On some numbers Duster would be accompanied by Top Topham on guitar, Stella Sutton on vocals and Tony Mills on bass. Also a certain "Peter Blue" played Fender 6-string bass that night. Peter Blue, of course, was Peter Green. "

The live session yielded the album's title track and Duster's third single - "Bright Lights, Big City". The Blue Horizon recording unit was set up in the gents loo.

According to Martin Celmins, the basis of Tony's one-man band big sound was a 1952 Gibson Les Paul Gold Top. The Gold Top was a gift to Duster from Peter Green, who previously had been given it by Eric Clapton.

"It was half busted," Peter recalls "when I got it from Eric. I went to his house in the forest a few times and noticed it there. I think one

MORE VENUES AND LIFESTYLES

of the pick-ups was missing and I said something like I could use that to smash up on stage like Jimi Hendrix and Pete Townsend, so Eric said I could have it. When Duster saw it he said it looked just right for his one-man band act. He liked it so much that I gave it to him and he had it fixed."

Soon after he acquired it from Peter in 1968, he had a mishap on stage at The Angel Hotel: the guitar was left propped against a chair and fell to the floor causing damage to the machine heads. Jim Cook volunteered to get him a replacement and raced off to borrow a white Telecaster from Vin Godier, another member of Jim's Whisker Davies band.

"After his performance, he was off to another gig at Middle Earth in London. He sadly died in a car accident a few years later, on the cusp of greater recognition. His recordings are still popular. He often joined Fleetwood Mac on stage, and tried unsuccessfully to stop Jeremy Spencer singing outrageous lyrics. He went on tour to America, extensively supporting John Mayall.

"Jacques Burnell, who attended The Royal Grammar School at Guildford, used to pose on his Harley Davidson right outside The Gin Mill entrance. His parents owned the 'Little Thatch' restaurant on Mead Row. He joined The Stranglers and their first rehearsal was in the Shalford Scout Hut."[1]

A feature of the late 1960s nationally was cross fertilisation of musicians between groups - the so-called super groups such as Cream and Blind Faith. Even locally, there appeared to be a looser feel to the group scene. Musicians such as Kirk Riddle and Dick Forcey, although having been associated with bands such as The Shakers, were now combining with others on an ad hoc basis. There is an advertisement, for example, for a concert at The Borough Hall,

---

[1] The Stranglers formed in 1974 were first known as The Guildford Stranglers.

GUILDFORD - THE ROCK'N'ROLL YEARS

Spirit Level, 1968

Back row: Julian Davies – keyboards *(Whisker Davies Blues Stormers)*, Ian May – vocals *(Grapes of Wrath, Market)*, Chris Brayne – drums *(Market, replaced Dick Forcey Stormsville Shakers)*, Roland Vaughan – tenor sax *(Hogsnort Rupert Band)*.

Front Row: Jim Cook – bass guitar *(Grapes of Wrath, Whisker Davies Blues Stormers)*, Dave Howard – alto sax *(Bizarre, later to play in the Graham Bond Organisation)*, Kevin Smith – guitar *(Electic Blue, replaced Ivor Shackleton Stormsville Shakers)*

Spirit Level Card, 1968
Design: Jim Cook

MORE VENUES AND LIFESTYLES

Godalming featuring such as The Graham Bond Organisation but including the "combined forces of Kirk Riddle, Dick Forcey, Whisker Davies, Ian May (vocals) and Powerhouse Jake". Kirk and Dick also played for a while in Spirit Level, the band formed in 1967 by Ian May and Jim Cook (bass guitar). This was a seven or eight piece R & B band, which supported such notables as Mott the Hoople, P. P. Arnold, The Nice, Fairport Convention, Graham Bond and Alexis Korner. Ian also played harmonica and sang with Champion Jack Dupree on a live session for Blue Horizon Records in 1968. Prior to this, Jim Cook had been involved with The Whisker Davies Blues Stormers, featuring drummer Pete Newberry, also founder of The Godalming Gin Mill Club.

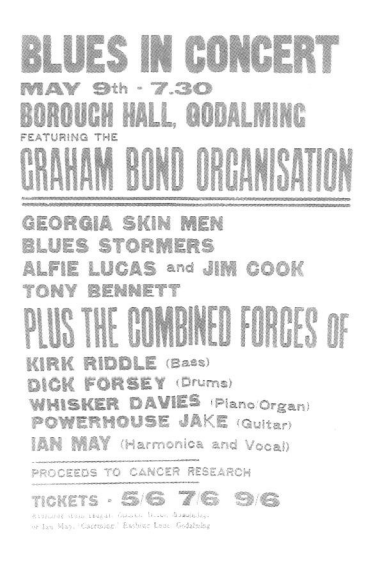

BLUES IN CONCERT
MAY 9th - 7.30
BOROUGH HALL, GODALMING
FEATURING THE
GRAHAM BOND ORGANISATION

GEORGIA SKIN MEN
BLUES STORMERS
ALFIE LUCAS and JIM COOK
TONY BENNETT

PLUS THE COMBINED FORCES OF
KIRK RIDDLE (Bass)
DICK FORSEY (Drums)
WHISKER DAVIES (Piano/Organ)
POWERHOUSE JAKE (Guitar)
IAN MAY (Harmonica and Vocal)

PROCEEDS TO CANCER RESEARCH
TICKETS - 5/6 7/6 9/6

The King's Head

The King's Head in Quarry Street is a timber framed building, dating from the early 17th century. It originally consisted of two adjacent houses, at some time knocked into one. It is a Grade II Listed Building in a conservation area and in the cellar there are what seem to be the foundations of a square corner tower of the castle's former outer wall, which once ran down Castle Street and along Quarry Street.

Although not primarily a live music venue for most of the sixties, certainly by 1970 this was in use as such when David Reading and Tony Backhurst appeared there, amongst other venues, firstly under the name of Bar X and then King Harvest. David wore his Davy Crocket hat and Tony his leather jacket and with their long hair they played acoustic guitars, harmony vocals and sang "hippy/protest stuff" (David's words).

Mick Douglas recalls an amusing incident when he was playing at the Kings Head with Dick Middleton, Greg McGregor and Tony Backhurst.

"They didn't have a licence for bands and there was a bit of a kerfuffle when we were playing there. It was getting late and the police raided the place. I threw my guitar down and ran out the door. A policeman grabbed me and my reply was that I had come to complain about the noise! He said 'Oh, sorry sir' and let me go. I shot off and picked my stuff up the next day!".

MORE VENUES AND LIFESTYLES

The Cygnet

A regular gig for Stuart Reffold and The Rivals and other groups was The Cygnet (run by a certain Pete Trim), a coffee bar by the river in Millbrook. This consisted of a series of rooms and Stuart remembers the place being

"full of beatniks. In the middle room there was a Bel Ami juke box, belting out John Lee Hooker and other great stuff. This was a very small venue.

"We used to go down The Britannia and get pissed. When we came back to The Cygnet to play, we were told to turn the music up (!)"

It was part of the beatnik scene, although Dave Reading refers to it as being post-beatnik (see on). The beatniks were the predecessors to the hippies - all long hair and beards. They graduated from trad music in the fifties to blues in the sixties. They preceded (and were a separate group from) the mods and rockers.

They were, in some cases, associated with drugs. Even at this early stage, everybody seemed to know somebody who had taken drugs, although the number involved was very limited. They certainly played no big part in the music scene until the mid to late sixties.

Dave Reading was with The Surrey Advertiser and one of his roles was as an occasional musical columnist. Around 1964 he formed a group which became known as The Crow Janes, whose line up comprised John Drinkwater and David on guitars, Tony Backhurst (vocals), Alan Bowly (drums), Tim McOnegal (harmonica) and Steve Hughes (bass).

The Crow Janes used to practice at the City Café in Onslow Street, which was run by Dave's granddad. They were influenced by Buddy Guy and Big Bill Broonzy and were the first electric band to perform at The Cygnet. Other gigs for them included The Harvest Moon, but a little later on they disbanded when Tony went travelling to Sweden. David says

"I first visited The Cygnet around the age of 15 or 16 and I was awe struck by the dingy, post-beatnik Davy Graham atmosphere. It felt cool to be seen as part of the Guildford scene with everyone sitting on the floor. One of those who attended was Lester Thomas, the coolest man in town, whose girlfriend was Margaret Collard.[1]

"The Cygnet closed around the mid-sixties when it was suddenly announced 'we are all now going to go up The King's Head'."

Tony Backhurst was interested in blues from a very early age. In fact, the first album which he acquired at age 12 in 1960 was a blues compilation, featuring Howlin' Wolf and other blues heroes. The Crow Janes were named after the Sonny Terry and Brownie McGee track "Crow Jane".

Dave Reading

♫♫

---

[1] Margaret has kept up her affiliations to the Guildford music scene by recently setting up home with Goff, formerly of The Bumblies.

MORE VENUES AND LIFESTYLES

Perhaps for reasons of modesty or to protect their loved ones, musicians are generally loathe to talk about their sexual exploitations. The subject of illicit sex was brushed under the carpet from the Victorian era, but had certainly begun to come out into the open by the 1960s. Perhaps partly due to the advent of the female contraceptive pill, this decade became known as "The Swinging Sixties". Whether or not this is a fair description is a moot point. Most teenagers' parents certainly had strict morals. Generally they would not allow their offspring to sleep with members of the opposite sex (or even the same sex come to that!). Sexual experimentation therefore had generally to be covert. Any suggestion that a couple were sleeping together or having sex meant in the eyes of the parents that they should get married. Even by the late sixties, members of the opposite sex living together before marriage was unusual.

Apart from the changing morals and music around this time, there was also a revolution in dress and style. Long hair and flowery shirts had become the norm. The film "Easy Rider" showing the attitude to long-haired hippies by the red necks in the southern states could just as easily have applied in England.

Author's note: *I remember from my days with The Switch, on the way to a gig, walking into a pub near Farnham. We walked in one or two at a time. The first one or two of us got served, but by the time all five of us had arrived, the landlord thought enough was enough of the long hair and the rest of us were denied service. This ended in a protest by Stuart Reffold of pouring his whiskey into an ashtray (what a waste - but worth it to make the point) and we all walked out.*

Stuart also recalls a time when he was with his dad, Charles, on the way to the Wrecclesham British Legion and stopped off for a drink, as his dad always did, at The Donkey. When they walked into the pub together, the welcome from the landlord was "Charles, is this young man with you? Well you know my rules. We can't have somebody coming in here with hair like that." To which Stuart replied "What are

157

you talking about. Are we going back to the Dark Ages?". The upshot was they never got served. Fortunately, the British Legion at Wrecclesham was a bit more liberal, where a good time was had by all.

Eric Clapton was resident in the Cranleigh area from the late 1960s. Terry Ward recalls seeing Ginger Baker in Cranleigh High Street around this period.

"They used to turn up in a psychedelic mini and hop into the cake shop, buy a load of cakes, and drive off. They wore outrageous clothes. They were a bit advanced for Cranleigh at that time".

An incident is recorded in hilarious detail in The Guildford and Godalming Times of 18th August, 1967 as follows:

"A small group of "flower people" descended on west Surrey over the weekend and scandalised residents near Winkworth Arboretum at Hascombe by bathing in the nude in the lake there.

"A nearby resident, who asks that her name and address should not be printed, told a reporter that she was in a room of her home overlooking the lawn when she saw a party of 5 or 6 young people.

"They said 'Can you help us?'. The men had long hair and beards. Ugh! Revolting types. They gave the sick girl a flower.

"One of the men told me the girl on the stretcher was his wife and that they had been married by flowers - whatever that means" he added.

♪♪

The Switch's manager, Don Backhurst, also managed other bands including those in which his son, Tony, performed. Don was in all respects a great character on the Guildford scene, he was 40 years old in the mid-sixties but was always seen with a very attractive young woman on each arm. David Rose of the Surrey Advertiser says:

"Don was often seen at the free festivals at the University of Surrey

MORE VENUES AND LIFESTYLES

in the 1970s. The first time I clapped eyes on him was at one of these festivals. It must have been 1975. I was walking up the stairs to the bar when Don came down. He had two stunning blondes hanging off each arm. 'Bloody hell,' I said to myself, 'who is he?' As a scruffy 15-year-old, I was amazed that this wrinkly old man could pull two gorgeous birds who were only a few years older than me."

As one of the great Guildford characters, it is worth spending some time on Don's background. He was, of course, a generation before most of those who appear in this book, but this perhaps adds a little spice and variety.

Don took part in the D-Day landings. After the war, he worked at Hepworths (the fifty bob tailors) in Guildford High Street, where he eventually became the Manager. He was also a life guard at The Lido. In the 1950s he set up in business selling second-hand cars from his family home in Worplesden Road, Stoughton. His son, Tony, remembers that as a boy he had the job of cleaning them, but such was the condition of some of the early ones that he was told not to stand on the running boards in case they collapsed!

One of Don's early ventures into music was through a fellow employee at Hepworths - Peter Arthur. Don managed The Leopard Spots, the skiffle group also featuring Bert Curtis. In Tony's words:

"My Dad had the gift of the gab. He was very charming, particularly with women. He had contacts in the music business, although he never played an instrument and, as far as I know, had no particular talent for music. He just knew all the right people in London in the swinging sixties and even the swinging fifties!"

By 1966 Tony Backhurst was living in Amsterdam. Don visited him and while there embraced all the ideals of the swinging sixties. He grew his hair and together they set off and explored Europe. When he returned he moved to Godalming and continued the car sales business. He was often seen cruising with friends in his Ford Galaxy convertible American car. In later years he pursued a modelling career, appearing in films and on T.V. In Don's words "I guess you'd call me an old hippy. I get a few looks when I'm out and sometimes people giggle. But it doesn't bother me, I'm a rebel." (Obituary by David Rose, published in the Surrey Advertiser August 27th, 1999).

Tony, by his own admission, had a somewhat confused upbringing. His mum left when he was very young. His dad had a string of girlfriends half his age, and Tony had spells living with his dad and his gran. One of his first jobs was working in the City, commuting up and down to town in his suit. Weekends were, however, a different matter. Tony became part of the "head" or "ravers" scene. This was the period between the beatniks and the hippies, but very much a part of that continuum. Tony was, in fact, a weekend raver and spent his whole weekend down at the river, either at The Cygnet or on Beatnik Island. His Dad or Gran or whoever it was he was living with at the time certainly did not worry if he was out all weekend, perhaps one advantage of his unconventional bohemian upbringing.

At that time the small island on the river opposite The Cygnet was overgrown and they used to camp there. Sometimes they went off to a posh party - not exactly as gatecrashers, but probably as friends of friends. There were no reports of significant damage by gatecrashers - probably the occasional spilt drink or cigarette burn - drugs were little in evidence although dope was smoked (purple hearts were for the mods). It was all about the music and the revolution.

Guildford was certainly a centre for travellers - bikers, etc. It is the confluence of a number of major roads and had the attractions of the river scene and plenty going on - the most in Surrey outside the Richmond/Kingston area.

Tony of course grew his hair. He was, however, concerned about his clothes and used to go up to London for his jeans and jean jackets - these could not be obtained in Guildford at the time. Many from Guildford used to travel up to the annual Richmond jazz festival (which later moved to Windsor and then Reading). By this time it was

MORE VENUES AND LIFESTYLES

not in fact a true jazz festival, mainly featuring groups such as The Who.

The Crow Janes was only a relatively small part of Tony's life. After about a year of working in the City, he had the yen to travel. He took his mate and his guitar over the Channel - his first trip abroad.

The money he took was a fiver (a reasonable sum of money in those days). In Tony's words he was "well looked after abroad". He spent nothing and brought back that fiver with him. Being English and with his long hair and guitar, he was welcomed everywhere. Tony never had any problems hitch-hiking in those days. The British flag and the guitar were a sign that he was welcome to a lift - not the opposite. Many times he got invited back to someone's house for food, bed and possibly more!

Tony was undoubtedly an adventurer. He seems to have made his principal income through music in the 1960s and early seventies, but not necessarily being in a permanent recognised band for much of the time. As a solo singer with his guitar and harmonica his gigs during the seventies included such prestigious venues as The Flamingo and The Marquee. He joined up with various bands when travelling in Germany and Sweden.

Don Backhurst photos

Tony Backhurst.

He was a singer/songwriter in the folk idiom, possibly somewhat similar to Donovan and wrote some of his own music when involved in the peace movement. During one of his long excursions in Amsterdam, he got remanded for misdemeanour on board somebody else's boat and his Dad came out to rescue him. Don then discovered that he too liked the lifestyle. There was one famous occasion when, driving around in his open top Ford with Tony playing the guitar and drinking, they nearly ran over a policeman. Tony's memory of how they got out of that little matter is a bit vague. As they say, "if you can remember the sixties you weren't there".

Chapter 9
Primevals and The Phantom Four

If Guildford had a small-town, sweaty equivalent of The Cavern, it was the Charlotteville Youth Club. There were also many pretenders to Guildford's equivalent to the early Beatles, including The Primevals and The Phantom Four.

The Charlotteville Youth Club was based in Sydenham Road (and the building is still there). Sydenham Road runs parallel to the High Street, but behind and south of it on higher ground and the youth club was approached down steps as if towards a basement.

Yet another of the many competitions of the period, this time The Guildford Beat Group contest was staged in May 1964. There were three heats and one was held in the Charlotteville Youth Club. The contestants in this heat included The Primevals and The Cutaways.

Author's note: *I was there in the audience of this heat, having appeared with The Weysiders in one of the other heats. I always thought "what a great atmosphere" of this particular club.*

The lead guitarist, vocalist and main man in The Primevals was Bruce Roberts. On Harmony rhythm guitar, but occasionally changing over to maracas or tambourine, was Colin Telling. Alan Franklin (Frank) was on the drums and Geoff Andrews on Framus bass guitar. Both Geoff and Colin contributed to the vocals. As the name implied, The Primevals had something of a primitive sound. That's not to say unsophisticated, but certainly exciting, Frank and Colin on maracas somewhat manic and Bruce who could never keep still. In the heat, the Primevals went down a storm and needless to say, by popular demand, moved through to the final of the competition.

♪♫

GUILDFORD - THE ROCK'N'ROLL YEARS

Geoff Andrews was born in July 1946 in Bristol, but his family moved to Guildford in 1950. From the early 1950s they lived in Leas Road and Geoff attended Sandfield Primary School in York Road.

The Leas Road area has now changed out of all recognition. This area has given way to the leisure centre and Law Courts where once stood the gasworks.

From the age of 11 onward, Geoff attended Stoke School in Markenfield Road (now demolished). It was here that he met the other future members of The Primevals. In fact, they were all in the same class - quite an extraordinary coincidence for four talented musicians. The school was located behind the Stoke Hotel. Bruce lived in nearby Linden Road, off Recreation Road by the sports ground.

Geoff learned to play the guitar at age 14 and like so many others was influenced by the likes of Lonnie Donegan and Eddie Cochran, but also Bert Weedon and Hank Marvin. He received his first guitar as a Christmas present. His family antecedence in the music business includes his cousin, who was a modern jazz musician and played at such venues as The Tunsgate Club.

Bert Weedon was one of the first people to popularise the electric guitar in this country and wrote the book with the somewhat improbable title "Learn to Play in a Day". He was not a rock'n'roller, being too old and too staid for that. He recommended that a guitarist should remain still and not move around while playing (a trait he also shared with Lonnie Donegan). Hank and The Shadows were exciting instrumentalists in this country (our equivalent of the American group, The Ventures) and they had certainly developed some on-stage moves with and without Cliff Richard.

The four members of the future Primevals attended the Methodist youth club in North Street and their first attempt at a group with electric guitars was known by the somewhat unusual name of Lance Prance and The Circulators.

Alan, who by this time was a junior reporter with one of the local

PRIMEVALS AND THE PHANTOM FOUR

papers, came to the conclusion that the name Lance Prance and The Circulators was not one to be reckoned with, but that The Primevals was. The Circulators did not have a bass guitarist and it was at this stage that Geoff decided to switch to playing bass. He acquired a semi-acoustic Framus bass, which he still has to this day.

Geoff left school in 1961 to become an apprentice mechanic. The rest stayed on for a further year to leave the secondary modern as they would have to at the age of 16 in 1962. Alan went to college, the remainder started work.

The Primevals was formed in 1963. Their first gig was at a Hallowe'en party at Burpham Village Hall. The group was short of equipment at this stage. As they had more than one vocalist, more than one mic stand was needed. The other stand, however, was formed from a broomstick (appropriate for Halloween) which they found backstage, nailed it to the floor, tied it to the ceiling and to the mic!

Geoff admits that they were not particularly good at this stage and throughout the latter part of 1963 they rehearsed and by January 1964 they were truly ready to gig. As they were working lads, they could afford to upgrade their equipment. Geoff had by now blown out the speakers of his little Watkins bass amp and thought it was time to

165

acquire the real mccoy, the Vox bass amp. As all guitar connoisseurs will know, the Vox amps were the business. There was no real competition at that stage, although Selmer, and later Marshall, produced good amps.

The original Primevals 1964. Alan Franklin (drums), Colin Telling (rhythm guitar), Geoff Andrews (bass) and Bruce Roberts (lead guitar and lead vocals).

More of The Primevals.

For a 17-year-old apprentice, earning 5 guineas a week, there was no alternative but the HP (hire purchase) system. Spread over a number of years, the weekly or monthly payments were relatively small and for a semi-pro band could be paid out of gig income. The Vox amps were so good that it was possible to perform without a PA, with three Vox amps each supporting a mic and one guitar through separate channels. I can vouch that the sound was good.

During the early part of 1964, The Primevals gigs included at The Alby John School of Dancing, The Godalming Angel, The Tunsgate Club, The Cygnet, Bellfields Youth Club and, in April 1964, the Guildford Civic Hall. The latter was as a support band, but would certainly have put The Primevals on the map as being one of the premier Guildford groups. A typical gig fee was £8, £2 each. This was good money for a night's work bearing in mind apprentices wages. Even an adult labourer was only earning £10 a week at this time.

Geoff remembers The Primevals as being a hard drinking band, but not into drugs. "After a gig" he says "we would be dropped off at the roundabout by the lido, clamber over the fence, get stripped off and jump into the pool. This was after midnight. The place was crowded!".

The Surrey Advertiser of the time refers to the Beat Group competition in the following terms:

"The first round of the Guildford & District Big Beat Competition, held in Charlotteville Youth Club on Whit Monday, was won by a Guildford band, "The Phantom Four" - by only three votes. The group had to compete against two other groups, The Elektrons from Camberley and The E-Types from Woking.

"About 150 young people, including of course some members of the Charlotteville Youth Club, turned up to vote for their favourite group. Charlotteville's leader, Mr. Brian Muggeridge, and his wife counted the votes at the end of the evening and found that The Phantom Four had three votes more than The Elektrons.

"The winning group will now go forward to the big final at Racks Close on June 6th. (In fact, due to adverse weather, the final was held at Charlotteville Youth Club).

"Tomorrow (Saturday) the second round of the competition - which is being organised by Richard Mott in aid of the Council of Youth Jazz Festival - will be held at St. Nicolas' Hall, Mill Mead, and groups competing will include The Nighthawks, The Weysiders, Ad Finitum and The Freeways."

A later edition of the paper reports the final in the following terms:

"Popular winners of Guildford's Beat Group Contest, finals of which were held at Charlotteville Youth Club, Sydenham Road, on Saturday night, were The Phantom Four.

"After playing non-stop for an hour before an audience of several hundred teenagers, the group walked away with the honours and £25 prize money, beating rival groups The Primevals and The Nighthawks.

"The Primevals were close runners up and received £10 prize money, while The Nighthawks who finished third, were awarded £5.

"Judges at the contest were Mr. Michael Owen (Surrey Advertiser reporter), Miss Merina Madeswick (record store sales girl) and Miss Pat Knight (newspaper reporter)."

There may have been some controversy about the judging of the competition at various stages. However, from the reports and photographs in the paper at the time, The Primevals certainly obtained good coverage from this competition, despite their runners up status.

PRIMEVALS AND THE PHANTOM FOUR

According to Geoff: "There was fierce competition. We were all young lads. Everyone had an ego. We were friends and we knew each other, but we all wanted to get on the gravy train. We were the sixties punks. We kicked arse. We did not conform to anything. The Phantom Four were smart. We hated them. The rivalry was intense."

Typical Primeval songs at this stage involved harmony singing, mainly between Bruce and Geoff, as for example, "Fortune Teller", "Eight Days A Week" and "You Really Got A Hold On Me". Other numbers particularly featuring Colin Telling on harmonica, maracas or tambourine included "Mojo", "Bo Diddly" and "Hog For You".

At the end of 1964, girlfriend pressure caused Colin to leave the group. Many group meetings and discussions followed and it was decided to continue as a three piece. Over the next few months, Bruce from time to time had ideas of re-expanding to a four piece, possibly by the addition of keyboards, but Geoff was adamant. "It's working as a three piece. If it ain't broke, don't fix it".

Bruce continued his day job as a salesman and the band came under the agency of DWG Entertainments (Mick Douglas, Lionel Webb and Mick Gurney). The gig list expanded. The geographical area in which they played also expanded. They did, however, have residences, in particular at The Harvest Moon.

Sunday night was a relatively quiet club night at the Moon and this was the resident gig for The Primevals at this time. In fact, in 1965 they were the longest running resident band at this club, both on Fridays and Sundays, and also had a residency at The Wooden Bridge supporting such acts as Reg Dwight (Elton John then playing keyboard with Steam Packet), Rod Stewart, Jeff Beck, Peter Green, John Mayall, Jethro Tull, Ten Years After, Sonny Boy Williamson, Graham Bond, Chicken Shack and The Herd. That's some list.

Despite being a three piece, The Primevals by now had a fairly full sound. Bruce had acquired a top of the range semi-acoustic electric guitar, a Gretch Countryman, which filled out the sound. As well as his lead work, he was a good rhythm player, essential for all guitarists in three-piece bands. The Primevals promotional literature of the time proclaims "A three-piece but no trio. All enquiries to the Ministry of Noise" and gives a Guildford 5-digit telephone number.

By the end of 1965 the band was expanding its repertoire to such numbers as "Turn On Your Love Light" by Bobby Bland, "Wade in the Water" by Ramsey Lewis, "Louisiana Hannah" by Larry Williams and the type of progressive numbers that the Graham Bond Organisation were known for. In 1966 the boys were looking for a new drummer, more in line with the type of music they were now playing and happened upon Dick Forcey, an old school buddy of theirs and ex of the Stormsville Shakers.

The Primevals finally disbanded in December 1966. Bruce wanted to turn pro. Geoff was still doing his apprenticeship at Haslemere Motor Co. (later to become Wadham Stringer) and could not finish this until the age of 21, which would be 1967 (although he had completed his exams at Guildford Tech a year earlier).

However, Bruce was impatient and in early 1967 left for London to form The Quik. Geoff recalls that he and Dick Forcey went round to Bruce's place for a rehearsal, only to be told by his Mum "he's gone to London to form a band".

By the early seventies, Bruce had appeared on The Old Grey Whistle Test in such company as Alan Bown and Jess Roden.

Geoff on the other hand in early 1967 had to remain local and semi-pro. He had a short stint with a three piece known as The Other Two Thousand, whose other members were Tony Boast (ex-guitarist with Ad Finitum) and Pete Anderton of Anderton's music shop fame.

In late 1967 Geoff met up with Stuart Reffold and the other members of The Switch in The King's Head in Quarry Street to take over as lead guitarist. It was also around about this time incidentally that he met his wife Linda. Unusually in the rock'n'roll business, Geoff and Linda have remained together over all the years, just having

PRIMEVALS AND THE PHANTOM FOUR

celebrated their 40th wedding anniversary!

THE
PRIMEVALS
"A THREESOME BUT NO TRIO"

ALL ENQUIRIES....

MINISTRY OF NOISE

GUILDFORD 63151

The Primevals as a three piece 1966. Geoff, Alan (behind) and Bruce.

Geoff at home 2008, with his original Framus bass.

171

Author's note: my diary shows that my group, The Switch, supported The Quik at the Godalming Heaven Club in May 1967. From September 1967 I was a student at Brixton School of Building, with digs near The Elephant & Castle. I used to meet Bruce near there, where he rehearsed in a pub in the New Kent Road. Around about that time, I also saw him with The Quik in Finchley. He regaled me of their trips to Iceland - the women and, of course, the drink.

♪♫

Andy Latimer came to prominence in the seventies for his work with Camel, but he also made a significant contribution to the Guildford music scene in the sixties, particularly through The Phantom Four, in conjunction with his brother, Ian.

Ian was born at St. Luke's Hospital in Guildford in March 1947, followed two years later, as was often the way, by a brother (Andy) in May '49. Their family lived in one of the prefabs in Pound Hill, Wood Street, until Ian was 11 years old, when they moved to Grange Road, Stoughton.

Ian passed his 11-plus and went to Pewley Grammar School, later to become part of George Abbot School. Andy became a pupil at Northmead Secondary Modern in Stoughton.

Their father had been a musician in a dance band during the war, mainly playing drums and keyboards. Ian remembers him playing the keyboards at home, particularly the Glen Miller type of stuff. Ian was more influenced by Lonnie Donegan, Tommy Steele, Elvis and later The Beatles. In a theme which is becoming familiar in this book, Ian studied Bert Weedon's "Play in a Day" (he wishes that title was true!) and with his brother formed a prototype skiffle group, which included Ian's mate from school, Richard Over. It was obvious, however, even in these early days that Andy had the greatest talent for the guitar and his father made the wise investment of arranging lessons for him.

PRIMEVALS AND THE PHANTOM FOUR

"Prior to that" says Ian "we had both had piano lessons. Unfortunately, these clashed with 5 p.m. prime time children's television and the piano lessons had to take second place. Andy learnt classical guitar. Over the years he continued to work on his guitar playing and still does."

From the prototype skiffle group of their early teens developed the classic beat group, The Phantom Four, around the end of 1963. The group consisted of Ian (bass guitar and vocals), Andy (lead guitar), Richard Over (rhythm guitar) and Andy's best mate from school, Alan Butcher (drums).

The Phantom Four's first gig was in January '64 at Rudgwick Village Hall. Ian recalls the fee being £5 and them all being plugged in to a single Watkins amplifier at the front of the stage. "There was no PA system" says Ian "but never mind the sound - all the girls were screaming and asking for autographs"!

Andy's early musical heroes were Hank Marvin, Buddy Holly, Keith Richards, Stevie Winwood, Eric Clapton, Peter Green, Jan Akkerman, Lennon and McCartney and Brian Wilson. "Our main

GUILDFORD - THE ROCK'N'ROLL YEARS

repertoire was The Shadows numbers. By 1964 we were doing The Beatles and The Beach Boys, Chuck Berry and Spencer Davis. Eric Clapton was a big influence."

1964 was, of course, *the* year of the beat groups and during the course of that year The Phantom Four acquired their trademark look and sound.

"Mum and Dad were right behind us" recalls Ian. "Dad was a good guarantor for the H.P., Mum made our black corduroy Beatle jackets. We often didn't get home until 2 a.m. and I'm sure they couldn't sleep until we were indoors".

The equipment consisted of Vox AC30 amps, cherry red Hofner Verithin guitars, and the dress code was Cuban-heeled boots, the Beatle jackets, blue shirts and maroon ties.

Andy was already over 6'4" and the 2" Cuban heels were an unnecessary appendage. Tottering through the hall at The Civic to get up on stage to perform, Ian insisted that the band were not seen with girlfriends, as this could affect their image. "We had a very professional set up" recalls Ian. "Suddenly there were a huge number of bands on the Guildford scene. We thought that around '64 the main three were The Stormsville Shakers as the big soul band, The

174

Primevals, the scruffy equivalents of The Rolling Stones, and us, the smart equivalent of The Beatles".

Richard Over only played a few gigs before Graham "Cupcake" Cooper took his place on rhythm guitar. Ian continues "By this stage there were three of us singing. We were doing harmonies, including songs by The Beatles, The Beach Boys and The Hollies".

The Phantom Four 1964. Richard Over (rhythm guitar), Ian Latimer (bass guitar and vocals), Andy Latimer (lead guitar), Alan Butcher (drums).

Asked about the so-called controversy over the '64 Beat Group Contest, Ian's reaction is that there was general rivalry between the bands, but probably more particularly between The Phantom Four and The Primevals. "I've always had a love/hate relationship with Geoff Andrews, even later on when we played together in 'Get Back'. This is nothing unusual in bands. It adds to the creative energy."

By late '64 the Phantom Four gigs were including local village halls, the Alby John School of Dancing and The Empire Ballroom in Bordon. Transport for any band could be a problem, but for the Four was organised by one Pete Greaves, who happened to have a decent van. He was effectively the fifth member of the band and paid an equal amount. Mr. Latimer Snr. was at this stage the manager, although they were later managed by Michael Crompton. Rehearsals were at the Spar shop in Worplesden Road, Stoughton, run by Richard's parents The demos were made at R. G. Jones Studio in Morden. Recordings included "Louie Louie", "A Certain Girl", "It's In Her Kiss", "Diddly Daddy", and "And I Love Her". The record was even on the juke box at the café opposite Barnes & Avis. This would have been the Continental Coffee Bar managed by Malverne Dann, who became a singer later in the seventies. In the year of 1965, this place was full of mods with all their Lambrettas outside.

Ian has particularly fond memories of what he terms the "debs dos", i.e. gigs where there were lots of posh women. He even wrote to Vogue and Queen magazines trying to get more gigs of this type, where one was always well looked after, well paid and able to perform to a good-looking audience. Ian recalls: "The band was generally well behaved. There were no groupies or drugs, but we had our little incidents - one band member who shall not be named, after his drumming left a little bit to be desired on that occasion - getting more and more pissed and eventually falling backwards on to the stage. Also the bread fights in the back of the van, much to the disgust of Pete the roadie."

Graham Cooper began life with The Phantom Four as a rhythm guitarist to replace Richard Over. However, when he returned to the group after some hospitalisation, they had apparently sold his Gibson guitar and replaced it with a Farfisa organ! Ian is not so sure that this is actually what transpired, but nonetheless the upshot was that Graham evolved into a keyboards player. Ian was the leader and also the lead singer. The others joked that he always made sure that he had the best mic. He acknowledged, however, that Andy and Graham were really the musicians.

PRIMEVALS AND THE PHANTOM FOUR

By the end of '65, the name Phantom Four had been shortened to The Phantoms. Now they were playing further afield, Hastings, Portsmouth and their biggest gig of all at The California Ballroom, Dunstable as support to Status Quo. The Quo had just had their first hit "Pictures Of Matchstick Men". At that stage they were not jean-clad. In fact, Ian's recollection is of them being a very smart group. The gig was before an audience of 1,600.

Throughout those years of the mid-sixties, Ian and his band colleagues always had the dream of making it big. Towards the end of '68, however, this dream had not materialised and Ian and The Phantoms played their last gig on a cruise on the river Thames.

There had been some slight tension within the band about the type of music to be played. Graham and Andy were moving more towards the Clapton blues type sound, whereas Ian and Alan were keener to retain the commercial harmony pop sound. The real reason for the break up, however, appears to have been a by now familiar story in this group, whereby one member (Andy) wanted to go pro, whereas others (Ian and Graham) had other priorities, including steady girlfriends with a view to marriage.

177

Andy and Alan continued as a three piece under the name of "Strange Brew", with one Doug Ferguson. Ian managed this outfit for a short while and he remembers one particularly stressful day in London doing the rounds of Apple Studios, Stigwoods and other record labels, trying to no avail to obtain a contract for The Brew. With regard to the recruitment of Doug Ferguson, Andy writes:

"We placed an advert for a bass player, to which Doug Ferguson responded. He was very solid and had some wonderful gear, including a Fender jazz bass, two Vox T60s and his own roadie. That was the formation of Brew in August 1968. After three months, Doug said he knew a much better drummer, so I went over to Epsom to see him. He was a rather unpromising looking 14- to15-year-old spotty teenager called Andy Ward, but he turned out to be a fantastic drummer! Alan (Butcher) was very good about it. It is always very difficult to make changes to a band.

"Brew's first gig was November 2nd, 1968, at The Four A's Club in Aldershot and Andy joined on November 10th. March 3rd, 1969, saw us passing an audition at The Marquee and on July 4th we played The Goldsmiths Art Festival with The Pretty Things, King Crimson, Strawbs, Groundhogs, Third Ear Band and Thunderclap Newman. Brew and Circus were probably the top Guildford groups at this time.

"We recorded six or seven pieces around this time, including 'Crossroads' and other Cream type things, but it wasn't going anywhere. Andy Ward left to join Shades, another blues band, while I joined up with an American bass player and a new drummer and recorded an album for a German producer under the name Abraham or something. Nothing ever came of it, it was never released.

"Doug had gone off to South Africa to play in a big band, but we kept in touch and eventually he came back, and Andy too, so we played for another year as a three-piece blues band until 1970.

"When we hooked up with Pete Bardens, he had four gigs booked in Ireland, but no band. We went to Ireland after only one week of rehearsals and played a mish mash of stuff. The Irish gave us a fantastic reception, because they were starved of bands. We decided we had to come back with a new name for the band - but we didn't! Eventually, either Doug or I came up with the name Camel.

"We joined up with Phillip Goodhand-Tait in June 1971. We were supposed to be a band and we did the Goodhand L.P., but Phillip wasn't a stage performer, so after that there wasn't enough going on."[1]

The Surrey Advertiser 30th May, 2003, reports:

"When The Brew finally split, Andy Latimer and Doug Ferguson went on to form Camel - a progressive rock band that was huge in the U.K. in the 1970s. Camel had a big hit in 1975 with the instrumental album "Snow Goose", inspired by the book of the same name by Paul Gallico.

Andy is still writing and playing with Camel, who are now based in the U.S.A. Graham Cooper has gone on to play guitar with other top musicians, including Ripley-born guitar legend, Eric Clapton."

Ian acknowledges that Andy was the musician of the brothers, although Ian himself was more of a front man, or rather had the front to get up and perform. Whereas Andy went on to musically greater things, Ian gave up the guitar for 30 odd years and did not perform again until he formed with Geoff Andrews a group around the years 2001/2, "Get Back". Ian, of course, performed at the famous 2003 Civic Hall Reunion gig and now admits that he "misses the buzz of playing".[2]

---

[1] Based on an original appreciation of Camel by Steve Hillyard and Alan Taylor's interviews with guitarist Andy Latimer, published in Pipeline year 2000.

[2] As at July 2008 Ian was now happily on his second marriage, living in delightful surroundings on the Surrey/Sussex border. Andy had battled health problems and was now living back in England in Bath. I had a brief telephone conversation with him for the purposes of this book and he seemed in very good spirits.

GUILDFORD - THE ROCK'N'ROLL YEARS

The original Camel (l to r): Doug Ferguson, Pete Bardens, Andy Latimer and Andy Ward.

Chapter 10
Switch from The Rivals

To illustrate the difficulties of obtaining musical equipment for youngsters and learning how to play, John Enever, who wanted to be a drummer, recalls at age 12 going to a music shop in Guildford, possibly Andrews, seeing a catalogue of pictures of drums and ordering a snare drum with cymbal on arm attached to the stand, then waiting ten weeks for this probably somewhat mediocre instrument to arrive. John was nonetheless now the proud owner of a "drum kit". A short while after this he purchased a bass drum which he had seen advertised and which turned out to be a large marching drum from The Salvation Army, which he put on the floor and attached a pedal and accessories such as cow bells. He then rushed home from school every day to practise the drums, listening to the records of The Shadows and trying to work out what drums were being played, having never at this stage seen the group in action and realising that there were other parts to a drum kit, including the tom-toms.

John's main early influence was indeed The Shadows' Tony Meehan, but later Ian Pace of Deep Purple, Buddy Rich, Ringo Starr (who John thought much underrated) and later still Ginger Baker with his double kit. He continued to develop his drum kit piece by piece and indeed was one of Pete Anderton's first customers (see chapter 6) when he went there with dad to purchase a proper small second-hand bass drum. One of the advantages of being a drummer was the ability to add piecemeal to the kit and it was not until much later in the late sixties that he acquired a full set of drums of the same make, being a Ludwig kit acquired from Chris Burrows of Circus.

Author's note: *through Wood Street cricket I met Pete Kately and*

GUILDFORD - THE ROCK'N'ROLL YEARS

through him Derek Cooper. In the autumn of 1963 we formed a band called The Trolls. Kately from Wood Street was a veteran at age 21 (!) and an excellent jazz guitarist to boot. I had to learn some interesting jazz chords to keep up with him on some of the unusual instrumentals we played.

The Trolls at Wood Street Village Hall, 1963.
l to r: Pete Kately, John Enever, Derek Cooper, Nigel Enever

Our gigs were limited, but we had a regular stint at the Wood Street British Legion. Being taller than average for my age, I found myself able to drink in pubs from the age of 15 without being questioned, a far cry from the ID now required of kids. Even brother John, aged 14, was the one to go to the bar to buy the drinks! Oddly, the snooker table was positioned between us and the audience. At least we got paid, even if it was only £2 per gig at the Legion (10 shillings or 50p each!). It could be argued that teenagers were better off drinking in the safe environment of a pub, than drinking unquantified measures of spirits at home, in the playground or market square. Teenagers being teenagers, they will drink.

By early 1964, The Trolls had run its course. Pete Kately was more interested in jazz and bassist Derek Cooper joined the police force and decided that this might not be compatible with playing in a group and The Weysiders were now formed.

The Weysiders were pretty small fry in the Guildford area, but playing in a group was an engrossing hobby for myself and many others of this period. One minute you could be doing some kind of humdrum job (or in my case being bored out of my mind in a law lecture), and the next you'd be up on stage - the hero of the moment and, if you were lucky, one or two girls looking on with possibly some immature teenage adulation, or was that glazed look one of astonishment that we could be that bad!

At St. Francis Church Hall. l - r: John Enever, Mick Welton (later to be replaced by Phil Henshall), Nigel Enever, Bob Cox and Julian Lyle. Julian was one of the temporary vocalists with The Weysiders. The other who gigged with them for a short period was Tony, later of the Smoke Stakks.

Chuck Berry, of course, was a great innovator and wrote his own material, but in this country those such as Lennon and McCartney were generally the exception to the rule in writing their own material. In common with other groups, The Weysiders had an extensive repertoire of covers; at the Cygnet, for example, playing three sets each of about 50 minutes and each containing 16 songs! This is a total of nearly 50 numbers, with scarcely a repeat. The quality may not have been great, but they certainly had quantity!

Author's note: *the discotheque had not yet been invented, but by the mid to late sixties the disco was beginning to be competition. We became members of The Musicians' Union (partly because they provided insurance for our instruments) and had car stickers with the exhortation "Keep Music Live".*

♪♫

A name still to be reckoned with on the Guildford music scene is that of young Stuart Reffold. I first met Stu when he was a pupil at Godalming Grammar School. He was in the first form and I in the fourth. At that stage he was already known for his ebullient personality and sporting prowess.

In 1963 The Rolling Stones came to Guildford. They appeared low down on the bill as part of a package tour and they had just had released the song "Come On". Stuart with his mates took himself off from the village of Elstead where he lived to Guildford Odeon to see The Rolling Stones on both this occasion and the next time they visited, at which stage they were a top of the bill band, having had chart success with "I Want To Be Your Man". Mick Jagger's style of singing and stage performance were an inspiration to Stu, who decided "that's what I want to be".

Around that time, aged 13, he formed a small group with school friends from Godalming Grammar and Meadrow Secondary Modern

SWITCH FROM THE RIVALS

School in Farncombe, called The Red Devils. They had one or two party gigs and this was the start of Stuart's singing career.

Stuart's musical talent was inherited mainly from his mother who was a singer, although could not afford the training to develop her career. Stu's father worked on Peter Seller's estate, a 16th-century period property, on the road to Cut Mill, near The Golden Fleece. This property was subsequently owned by Ringo Starr and then Stephen Stills, with Stu's dad still working on the estate.

Stuart's first proper group was The Rivals under manager Mike Dunn. There was an early line up of this, including Nick Dogget on drums and Bruce Bunting on piano (later to join The Whiskey Ring). This early line up had one or two gigs, including the Godalming Wilfred Noyce Youth Centre.

The Rivals. Roy Norris, Stuart Reffold, John Enever, Phillip (Joe) Hunter-Dunn, Pete Oliver.

GUILDFORD - THE ROCK'N'ROLL YEARS

The Rivals 1964.

Stuart Reffold in further action with The Rivals.

Author's note: *During the sunny summer of '63, I sat out in the grounds of Guildford Tech teaching my friend, Joe (Phillip) Dunn to play the guitar. He was about to become the bass guitarist in The Rivals.*

SWITCH FROM THE RIVALS

Joe Dunn was not averse to physical labour and had acquired the job of constructing a swimming pool for a fairly wealthy customer in Worplesden. This was when he recruited my brother John and myself to assist in the work. It was during this period that Joe approached John about joining The Rivals. John was flattered by the offer. He was only just 15 years old and in a group, The Weysiders, which appeared to be going nowhere and The Rivals were better established with more gigs on the horizon.

The established line up of The Rivals became Stuart Reffold on vocals, harmonica, tambourine and maracas, John Enever on drums, Peter Oliver lead guitar, Roy Norris rhythm guitar and Joe Dunn on violin bass. At a later stage the group reduced to a four piece with the omission of the rhythm guitar. Copies of the Surrey Advertiser of the period reveal that The Rivals had started regularly gigging and The Harvest Moon begins to feature large.

At this stage Stuart was still at school, but in his own words "I was launched out by the Headmaster, Mr. Dewar, for failing my exams". There is also some reference to a matter concerning the school Secretary and the tuck shop! Stuart's mind was evidently on other things, including the group.

Stu also recalls that:

"It was around this time that Mick Jagger was wearing a crew neck jumper and playing the tambourine. I followed suit. We played numbers like "Not Fade Away". There were plenty of gigs around, apart from The Harvest Moon, including village halls and tennis clubs, and we had a Sunday night spot at The Tunsgate Club. Although I was at school until 1965/66 and John was at school until the summer of '65, Pete Oliver had a good job with Cornhill Insurance, so some of the guys had the dough to buy the gear. Roy's dad worked at the clothes shop, Kinch & Lack, in Guildford."

The Rivals were certainly a very well set up group, organised by Mike Dunn, Joe's brother, at East Horsley. He perhaps had visions of

GUILDFORD - THE ROCK'N'ROLL YEARS

The Rivals being the second Beatles. He had good contacts in London and they played at The Bag o' Nails (supporting Scott Walker), The 100 Club, The Marquee and The Ram Jam Club in Brixton. The gear was taken up to London in the Commer van and John went up on the train from school with instructions on which underground trains to catch. In many cases, they did not start playing until 11 p.m.

♪♫

In 1965 The Whiskey Ring was formed. At this stage the line-up was Nigel Enever on lead guitar, Roger Thackray (formerly of The Rocking Crescendos) on bass guitar, Bruce Bunting on piano, Alan ("Bo") Bridle (formerly of The Secrets) on drums, and Tom Hogan on vocals, under the management of Graham Hawkins. For a short while in 1966 David Reading took over on lead guitar.

Author's note: *Tom was a very large man, about 6'4" tall as I recall. My memories of Tom are as a gentle giant. He wouldn't pick a fight, but you would certainly wish for him to be on your side if there was any trouble. I think the last time I had seen Tom prior to joining The Whiskey Ring was at Stoughton Juniors (he was one or two years above me there) and I was surprised now to see him in the role of a singer. However, he could certainly sing. He had a rich voice with perhaps something of the Tom Jones about it. The rest of us were by now true experienced and semi-pro musicians. Alan and Tom lived on Bellfields estate, Bruce in Farncombe, and Roger in East Horsley.*

The Whiskey Ring's gigs included the usual culprits, The Harvest Moon, The Wooden Bridge and Tunsgate Club and the song list ranged from Gershwin ("Summer Time" and "Fever", which were songs often performed by bands of that era) through Moz Alison to Jimmy Witherspoon. One of the problems was the piano, and The Whiskey Ring were not the only group to have had this problem. Bruce had to rely on there being a piano at each venue (and in those days this would be the norm), rely on that piano being in tune and then place a mic inside the piano for amplification - not ideal!

The Whiskey Ring in Stoke Park 1966.
l - r: Martin Jupp (behind) (organ), Alan Bridle (drums), Roger Thackray (bass), Tom Hogan (vocals), Nigel Enever (behind) (guitar).

After a few months, Bruce decided to leave the band and he was replaced by Martin Jupp. Although Bruce was an excellent pianist, the move had the advantage of Martin playing the Lowry organ, a close relative of the Hammond organ with Leslie speaker. The only downside to this was that it took four people to carry the organ from the van to the rehearsal room or venue stage!

During February 1967, Alan and Tom became restless and decided to leave the group. Tom got married on 18th February and later formed the group Soul Bucket. Alan decided to emigrate to Australia and the remnants of The Whiskey Ring (now including Richard Cayre on organ) had discussions with John Enever and Stuart Reffold of The Rivals about forming a new band, The Switch. in reference to the switch from The Rivals to The Whiskey Ring.

The Switch, Peasmarsh Village Hall 1967. Roger Thackray, John Enever, Nigel Enever, Richard Cayre, Stuart Reffold.

The new group commenced rehearsals at the same venue used by The Whiskey Ring, Peasmarsh Village Hall, and in early March visited Kings Road, Chelsea, to pick up some of the latest fashions. Flared trousers, flowery shirts and long hair were now the order of the day. This was after all to be the year of the summer of love. This was one of a number of visits to Kings Road and Carnaby Street. Lord Montague's Boutique opened in Guildford around now. Surely a sign of the times. Was Guildford to become the new Chelsea? - probably not.

Such spare time as there was was spent with girlfriends and old schoolfriends at such hangouts as The King's Head, Quarry Street. The form for many was to start off at The King's Head and then take a pipkin (large can of bitter) to whatever party was going on.

Also around this time Guildford's first true night club had opened - Dronfields, to replace the old Tunsgate Club. This was a disco with late night opening. Late night was probably 2 a.m. latest, but this was a big change on what had gone before. The Harvest Moon was essentially a live music club, whilst Dronfields was a disco.

Author's note: *one of my most memorable nights with The Switch was playing at London University's Royal Holloway College in Englefield Green, followed by an all-night session at The Harvest Moon - home at 6 a.m. On trying to exit Englefield Green, we had great difficulty finding John and eventually dragged him out of the flower bed, off a female fan! His nickname was after all "Nookie".*

By late August 1967 Geoff Andrews was starting to rehearse with the group, so there was a smooth changeover when he took my place and I started my degree course in the autumn. My last gig with The Switch was on Saturday, 9th September, at The Civic Hall supporting Circus. This is where my part in the story really ends. I was now a mere spectator, but continued to follow the fortunes of such as Circus, Phill Tate and The Switch.

♪♫

Geoff Andrews had by now reinvented himself as a lead guitarist (having played bass in The Primevals and The Other Two Thousand).

Author's note: *whether it was because Geoff had taken my place, or for other reasons, I shall never know, but The Switch now seemed to go from strength to strength!*

There were to be some other variations of personnel within The Switch, perhaps partly as a result of personality clashes. Around the autumn of '67 Richard, the organist, was to leave, not to be replaced. The music was still predominantly soul, but under Geoff's influence was now starting to move towards a heavier, more guitar-orientated sound.

During 1968 Ivor Shackleton joined The Switch. At one stage there were both Ivor and Geoff, at another stage Ivor and eventually just back to Geoff again as guitarist. Also around this time Don Backhurst became Manager with Ray Bradman as roadie.

SWITCH FROM THE RIVALS

Geoff says:

"Ivor brought a lot of professionalism to the group. He was immaculate. He looked good on stage. He was a tight guitarist.

"Ivor played the soul bits and I played the more progressive stuff. However, this led to a clash of egos, possibly due to having two lead guitarists in the group, and we were always at each other's throats. The crunch came when it was proposed that Don Backhurst be Manager. I remember we were playing at The Wooden Bridge and Stuart asked us through into the other bar to meet the new Manager. He was dressed in a white suit, with cowboy hat and boots and I thought 'no way is he going to manage me'.

"I decided to leave the band, or possibly I was given the push. They carried on just with Ivor for a few months and then I came back to take Ivor's place and to continue as a four piece, but to play more alternative type of music instead of soul. Stuart and I started writing stuff."

Don Backhurst could, in fact, have done great things for The Switch. He was a friend of Mike Hazlewood, who proposed to introduce them to the song "Little Arrows". By this time, however, there appears to have been some disillusionment with Don and the opportunity was passed up. The song subsequently went to Leapy Lee. The rest, as they say, is history.

John Enever feels that Don Backhurst was indeed very influential for the band and was perhaps not taken as seriously as he should have been. He tried to organise the band and indeed got them into recording at the excellent Radio Luxembourg studios in London. John's memory of turning down the "Little Arrows" song, was that they thought that this was bubblegum music. "We did not play this type of music. I am sure somebody else gladly did, but one makes mistakes along the way".

After Ivor left The Switch he formed The Groove with the remnants of Just Five. The personnel comprised Barry Wallis, Pete

Anderton, Dave Holt on keyboards, a sax player (Bob Webb), a bass player and Ivor on guitar. For a very short period after this, Ivor was in the Spirit Level with Jim Cook and Ian May. This, however, was a blues set-up which did not quite suit Ivor's style of playing. After Spirit Level, Ivor changed to playing bass with The Frank Alan Sound and then Sweet Charity, again with some ex-members of Just Five, including Dave Holt..

In 1969 The Switch signed up with a Portsmouth agency, which had to be on an exclusive basis for the work to be offered, which included gigs at The Lyceum at Weymouth, supporting such Top of the Pop acts as Amen Corner and The Equals. John recalls one gig at The Wooden Bridge as support to Rod Stewart/Jeff Beck when Stuart announced Jeff as "Geoffrey", much to Beck's annoyance.

The Switch had by now survived in various forms for the best part of three years and when they disbanded Geoff for his part did not pick up the guitar and play in a band again until 1995, when Terry Ward reformed The Bumblies. John, Roger and Stuart have played almost continually since that time in various bands, Stuart in particular in recent years with The Fugitives.

Prior to The Fugitives, Stuart played in various bands from the seventies onwards, including Duffy and had a solo career involving some songwriting. He had a short period out of music as a rep or tour guide with a travel company in Switzerland, following Duffy's musical success there.

One of the more memorable Switch gigs was a trip along the river Thames, which included the company of a number of models and The Switch's picture appeared on the front cover of the "In Britain" magazine. These were indeed the high days of the swinging sixties. Like many fashionable young men of the era, John Enever had a sports car and a mini. He dabbled in drugs, but was not heavily into them. He recalls hanging around with Ian Jelfs and smoking dope, but also being good mates with Colin Rigden, known as Pod, the

SWITCH FROM THE RIVALS

hairdresser from Anthonys of West One. Pod did not have a car and John drove him around and they visited various customer's houses and flats, including those of Eric Clapton in Ewhurst, John Squire of Yes and Keith Richards in Chelsea. In John's words

"Pod was a King's Head sort of guy. It was perhaps a case of us having to be seen with the right people - posing if you like - rather than for any particular profit for our music, although I can recall chatting about various venues and gigs with these famous guys. Anthony had an Aston Martin and became our Manager. Pod later worked at Sweeny Todds, the top hairdressers in Kings Road."

Ray Bradman was the roadie for The Switch in the late 1960s and, in fact, met his wife, Sue, at John's 21st in 1970. Sue used to go to The Plaza Ballroom dances. All the girls were in love with Pod. He was a great dancer. The floor would clear when he was dancing.

1968. Stuart Reffold, Roger Thackray, Ivor Shackleton,
Geoff Andrews, John Enever.

During the summer of 1969 The Switch made two cruise trips from Southampton to New York on the S.S. Aurellia, spending one day in

New York on each occasion and entertaining students from all over the world. Altogether they were professional for about one year. Although John had had to break his engineering apprenticeship at Drummonds to achieve this, even now the memories of that time made this well worthwhile. The Switch's last gig was on New Year's Eve 1969 at Pantiles (still going), a new club to have opened in Bagshot.

Geoff says:

"We had set ourselves a time schedule. We were all agreed that if we had not achieved all we had set out to achieve, i.e. a recording contract, by the end of 1969, that would be the end of the band."

Styles of music and fashions do not conveniently divide themselves into particular decades. The music of Chuck Berry and the fashions of Elvis Presley burst onto the scene in the mid-50s and continued to be an influence up till around the mid-60s, whereupon psychedelia took over. The flowery shirts and flared trousers were a feature of the late 1960s and early seventies. Nonetheless, around 1969/70 The Beatles folded, as did a number of the bands referred to in this book, including Circus, The Brew and The Switch. New Year's Eve 1969 was in some ways the end of an era. The swinging sixties had run its course.

♪♫

SWITCH FROM THE RIVALS

The Switch 1969.
Top: John Enever, Roger Thackray, Geoff Andrews.
Middle: Stuart Reffold, Geoff and Roger.
Bottom: Roger, Stuart and Geoff.

GUILDFORD - THE ROCK'N'ROLL YEARS

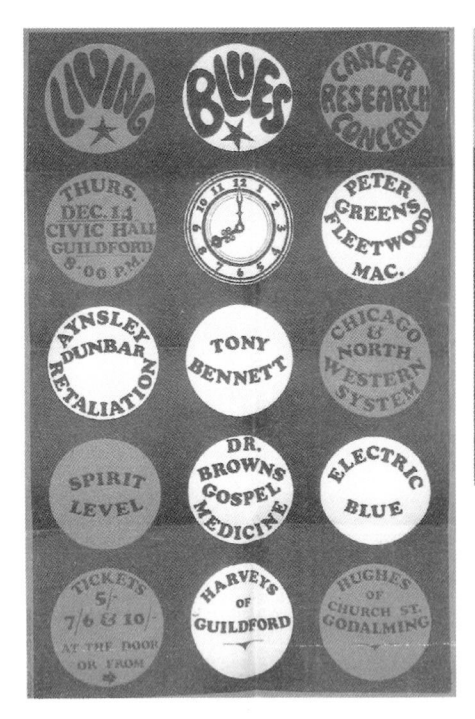

Duster Bennett, Godalming, 1968

Gin Mill Posters by Jim Cook including back cover